D0717332

MEMORIALS

MEMORIALS

An Anthology of Poetry and Prose

Edited by June Benn

Ravette London

First published 1986 by Ravette Limited

Printed and bound in Great Britain for Ravette Limited
3 Glenside Estate, Star Road, Partridge Green,
Horsham, Sussex RH13 8RA
by William Clowes Limited
Beccles and London

ISBN 0 948456 23 X

Dedication

In memory of Eddie, Sam and Gisela
whose passing gave the publisher cause
to reflect on our mortality

Acknowledgments

The editor gratefully acknowledges permission to reproduce the following copyright material:

Extracts from the Authorized King James Version of the Bible and the Book of Common Prayer of 1662, which are Crown Copyright in the United Kingdom are reproduced by permission of Eyre and Spottiswoode (Publishers) Limited, Her Majesty's Printer, London.

The following extracts from Greek and Latin authors appear in The Oxford Book of Death edited by D. J. Enright and are reprinted with the permission of the Oxford University Press: 11 lines from The Meditations of Marcus Aurelius, transl. A. S. L. Farquharson (1944); 3 lines from Seneca, translator and source unknown; 4 lines from C. M. Bowra's translation of 'Inexorable Death' by Aeschylus from 'Niobe' from the Oxford Book of Greek Verse in Translation edited by T. F. Higham and C. M. Bowra (1938); 4 lines from Epicurus: The Extant Remains translated by Cyril Bailey (1926); 14 lines from The Republic of Plato translated by F. M. Cornford (1941). The extract from the Zen Buddhist Bassui is also reprinted from The Oxford Book of Death – translator and source unknown.

POEMS
George Barker from Dreams of a Summer Night: Wild Dreams of Summer What is your Grief. Reprinted by permission of Faber and Faber Ltd., and John Johnson.
Laurence Binyon: an extract from 'For the Fallen' from 'The Four Years, 1919' and an extract from 'The Burning of the Leaves 1944'. Reprinted by permission of Mrs Nicolete Gray and The Society of Authors on behalf of the Laurence Binyon Estate.
Vera Brittain: 'Perhaps' and 'To my Brother' are included with the kind permission of the literary executors of Vera Brittain.
John Buchan: from 'Fratri Dilectissimo' from his book 'Montrose' with the permission of the Rt. Hon. Lord Tweedsmuir.
Sir E. K. Chambers: 'Lelant' (included in 'Poems of Today' – second series (Sidgwick and Jackson) published by the English Association), originally privately printed by the author: with the kind permission of the English Association.
G. K. Chesterton: from 'The Great Minimum' with the permission of Miss D. E. Collins.
J. M. Cohen: translator of lines translated from the Spanish, originally from the Nahuatl of Mexico in the Rider Book of Mystical Verse ed. J. M. Cohen (Rider) with the kind permission of the translator.
John Cornford: 'To Margot Heinemann' from 'John Cornford: A Memoir,' edited by Pat Sloan, reprinted by permission of the Estate of Pat Sloan, and Jonathan Cape Limited.

Siegfried Sassoon: 'Everyone Sang' by permission of George Sassoon.

Stevie Smith: 'Away Melancholy' from Selected Poems 1962. Reprinted by permission of James Macgibbon, the literary executor of the late Stevie Smith, and Penguin Books Ltd.

Dylan Thomas: 'Do not go gentle into that good night' reprinted by permission of J. M. Dent and Sons Ltd., the Trustees for the copyrights of the late Dylan Thomas.

Helen Waddell: a translation of Burial Song by Prudentius from 'Medieval Latin Lyrics' published by Constable Ltd., and by Penguin Books Ltd., and with the permission of Constable Ltd.

Arthur Waley: 'Shang Ya!' a Chinese oath of friendship, 'On the Death of his Father', and 'Two Burial Songs', from 'One hundred and seventy Chinese Poems', by permission of Constable Ltd., and Mrs Arthur Waley.

W. B. Yeats: 'Death' by permission of A. P. Watt & Son.

PROSE

A passage from Humboldt's Gift by Saul Bellow, is reprinted by permission of the Harriet Wasserman Literary Agency Inc. and A. M. Heath and Co.

E. M. Forster: 'What I Believe' from 'Two Cheers for Democracy' (1951) is reprinted by permission of Edward Arnold Publishers Ltd.

The letter from *Joyce Grenfell* to Lavinia Dyer is reprinted from 'Joyce by herself and Friends' by permission of Macmillan and Futura and Richard Scott Simon Ltd.

J. Krishnamurti: from the Penguin Krishnamurti reader; selected from 'The First and Last Freedom, Life Ahead and This Matter of Culture' originally published by Victor Gollancz. The passage is reprinted by permission of Victor Gollancz Ltd.

C. S. Lewis: The letters to his father dated 23 April 1921 and to Owen Barfield dated 18 May 1945 are reprinted by kind permission of Collins, publishers of The Letters of C. S. Lewis ed. W. H. Lewis and published by Collins in 1966.

Lin Yutang: translator and editor of 'The Wisdom of Laotse'. Published by Michael Joseph, London, and Random House Inc., New York and the copyright of Random House is reprinted by permission of Random House Inc., New York.

A passage from 'Death' by *Maurice Maeterlinck* translated by Alexander Teixeira de Mattos is reprinted by permission of Methuen & Co.

Phaedo: *Plato* (page 7–8) is from the translation by Hugh Tredennick (Penguin Classics ed. 1969) and is reprinted by permission of Penguin Books Ltd.

George Santayana: 'The Life of Reason', is reprinted by permission of the publishers Constable Ltd.

A passage from (ed.) *Arnold Toynbee* in 'Man's Concern with Death' is reprinted by permission of the publishers, Hodder and Stoughton Ltd.

Upanishads – the extract on page 212 is taken from the translation by Juan Mascaro (Penguin Classics 1965) by permission of Penguin Books Ltd.

Helen Waddell: the extract from a lecture 'Poetry in the Dark Ages' (1947) is reprinted by kind permission of The Glasgow University Press, and the Secretary of the University Court.

Ludwig Wittgenstein: 'Tractatus Logico Philosophicus' translated by C. K. Ogden is reprinted by permission of Routledge and Kegan Paul Ltd.

Arthur Waley: When Chuang Tzu's wife died . . . from 'Three Ways of thought in Ancient China' (1939) is reprinted by permission of George Allen and Unwin Ltd.

Seneca: 'De Consolatione ad Marciam' is reprinted by permission of William Heinemann Ltd., who published the translation of John W. Basore.

St Augustine: 'Confessions' translated by R. S. Pine-Coffin (Penguin Classics 1961) is reprinted by permission of Penguin Books Ltd.

Thomas à Kempis: 'The Imitation of Christ' translated by Leo Sherly-Price (Penguin Classics 1952) is reprinted by permission of Penguin Books Ltd.

Extracts from 'The Grace of Zen': Zen texts for meditation ed. Karlfried Durkheim and others by kind permission of Burns and Oates Ltd., and the Search Press, Tunbridge Wells.

I have been unable to discover the authorship of the poem on page 261 beginning 'Not, how did he die,' and apologise to the author and/or copyright holder. Every effort has been made to trace the authorship of any copyright material including translations of more than one line.

June M. W. Benn.

Introduction

Many people now die unsustained by Christian or any other religious belief, and are buried, or more often cremated, at services attended by mourners who may also be uncertain about their religious beliefs, or clear unbelievers. Most people however still wish for some ceremony to say goodbye and to close the chapter, when those they love die.

A Christian burial is given in this country (UK) unless it is specifically declined. A number of people do now request 'secular' funerals, and amongst certain sections of society Memorial Services are becoming more and more popular. But there is no reason why 'ordinary' funerals at crematoria, whether religious or not, should not also incorporate readings and music. The particular purpose of this anthology is to bridge the gap which is often felt to exist between the sometimes perfunctory ceremony and the wish to 'personalise' the funeral, to say goodbye with dignity, and also perhaps to concentrate the mind and meditate upon one's own life and life in general.

It is often only with great difficulty that the mourners – usually close family and friends – choose suitable passages to be read aloud at these services. There has been a general tendency in recent years to concentrate on the life as it was lived, rather than on its end. But at times of shock, grief, and preoccupation with the rites attendant upon death in our society, it is difficult for even the best-intentioned to find some adequate expression for feelings of loss, especially if there is no Church service. Words can be very helpful either read aloud or just read privately by individual mourners.

It is hoped that this anthology brings together some passages of poetry and prose which may be of use on these occasions and during the period of mourning. I have included the great passages, hallowed by time, of Jewish and Christian consolation. Whether taken in a religious context or not, they appeal to us all through the majesty of their language. English literature is imbued in any case with the spirit of the Bible, passages from which are of course used at a Christian burial. But a generation has grown up which has never heard the old Authorized Version – or the 1662 prayerbook – and which probably does not read poetry in the normal course of things.

I have tried to please different tastes and different attitudes to death and to present both the familiar and the new within the confines of a small book. I have also given a separate section of appropriate passages for atheists, agnostics, rationalists and humanists. Most extracts chosen are fairly short, not too complex to be taken in by the ear and suitable for reading aloud.

Passages of total despair, or railing at God or his absence, or affecting but maudlin pieces of the last century, are perhaps not quite right for funerals, though the expression of grief in words enables some people to contain their own grief, whilst others break down – which in this country is seen as embarrassing. There is ample choice therefore to suit different tastes. The present day Memorial Service tries to celebrate life in the midst of death rather than its opposite, unless the deceased believed, or the family believe in an after-life.

To some, even the thought of death is 'morbid' and approached if at all with reluctance and dread, like the writing of a will which is put off out of superstition. But even to these people, this book may I hope prove helpful as it has certainly been to its compiler. It is, after all, the mourners who need comfort whatever their religious beliefs, not the dead; it is the living who regard funerals with distaste, and even religious people may regard them as a necessary evil, if they believe the soul has already been taken care of. Some people, to spare their relatives after their own death, may wish to leave instructions for the kind of funeral they would wish and the passages they might like read at a Memorial Service, and blank pages have been left at the end of the book for this purpose or for the addition of favourite passages. Perhaps also the reading of some of the best expressions of thoughts about life and death may put our own lives into perspective, so that a funeral may not in the end be without some good result if we can do justice to the dead, and to ourselves. I have also added a number of very short quotations which might be suitable for silent meditation during a service, even a non-religious one, or as the text for an address by a minister or a friend.

The unsatisfactory nature of many 'mass-produced' funerals has recently been a matter of some disquiet to clergy themselves who have to officiate, and certainly to agnostics who dislike the often perfunctory nature of some funerals at crematoria. I hope this book may save believers and non-believers alike a little time and trouble over the organisation of funerals and Memorial Services and will help all kinds and conditions of men and women.

JUNE BENN

Table of Contents

Bright is the ring of words
When the right man rings them,
Fair the fall of songs
When the singer sings them.
Still they are carolled and said –
On wings they are carried –
After the singer is dead
And the maker buried.

R. L. Stevenson

1

Life and Death: The Body and the Soul

Animula, Vagula, Blandula,

O my little spirit, drifting gently away, the guest and the companion of my body, who will now depart to pallid, dreary and stark regions, leaving your familiar places. . . Let us just for one moment look together at a world which we shall probably never see again . . . and try together to confront Death with eyes open.

Emperor Hadrian, translated J. Benn

My little wandering sportful soul,
Guest, and companion of my body,
had liberty to wander through all places, and to survey
and reckon all the rooms and all the volumes of the
heavens . . .

John Donne: from *Ignatius, his Conclave*

They had their being together. Parts they are of one reasonable creature, the harming of the one is the weakening of the working of the other. What sweet contentments doth the Soul enjoy by the Senses? They are the Gates and Windows of its Knowledge, the Organs of its Delight. If it be tedious to an excellent Player on the Lute, to abide but a few Months the want of one, how much more must the being without such noble Tools and Engines be painful to the Soul? And if Two Pilgrims, which have wandered some few miles together, have a hearts-grief when they are near to part, what must the Sorrow be at the parting of Two so loving Friends and never-loathing Lovers, as are the Body and Soul?

William Drummond of Hawthornden:
from *The Cypress Grove*

The Venerable Bede in his Ecclesiastical History of the English People (*c.* 731 AD) wrote of human life thus: It seems to me O King that the present life of men on earth, when compared with the stretch of time unknown to us, is as if when in winter time you sit feasting with your chiefs and ministers . . . one little sparrow should fly swiftly through your hall, coming in at one door and flying out through another. . . . Soon returning to the winter from whence it came and vanishing from your sight, its flight is like Man's life; for of what went before, or what will follow, we are utterly ignorant. . . .

translated J. Benn

Poor soul, the centre of my sinful earth,
  My sinful earth these rebel powers array,
Why dost thou pine within and suffer dearth,
  Painting thy outward walls so costly gay?
Why so large cost, having so short a lease,
  Dost thou upon thy fading mansion spend?
Shall worms, inheritors of this excess,
  Eat up thy charge? Is this thy body's end?
Then, soul, live thou upon thy servant's loss,
  And let that pine to aggravate thy store;
Buy terms divine in selling hours of dross;
  Within be fed, without be rich no more:
    So shalt thou feed on Death, that feeds on men,
    And Death once dead, there's no more dying then.

William Shakespeare

Dirge for Fidele

Fear no more the heat o' the sun,
  Nor the furious winter's rages;
Thou thy worldly task hast done,
  Home art gone, and ta'en thy wages.
Golden lads and girls all must,
As chimney-sweepers, come to dust.

Fear no more the frown o' the great,
   Thou art past the tyrant's stroke;
Care no more to clothe and eat,
   To thee the reed is as the oak.
The sceptre, learning, physic, must
All follow this, and come to dust.

Fear no more the lightning-flash,
   Nor the all-dreaded thunder-stone;
Fear not slander, censure rash;
   Thou has finished joy and moan.
All lovers young, all lovers must
Consign to thee, and come to dust.

No exorciser harm thee!
Nor no witchcraft charm thee!
Ghost unlaid forbear thee!
Nothing ill come near thee!
Quiet consummation have,
And renownèd be thy grave!

William Shakespeare: *Cymbeline*

Before the Beginning of Years

Before the beginning of years
   There came to the making of man
Time, with a gift of tears;
   Grief, with a glass that ran;

Pleasure, with pain for leaven;
    Summer, with flowers that fell;
Remembrance fallen from heaven,
    And madness risen from hell:
Strength without hands to smite;
    Love that endures for a breath:
Night, the shadow of light,
    And life, the shadow of death.

And the high gods took in hand
    Fire, and the falling of tears,
And a measure of sliding sand
    From under the feet of the years;
And froth and drift of the sea;
    And dust of the labouring earth;
And bodies of things to be
    In the houses of death and of birth;
And wrought with weeping and laughter,
    And fashioned with loathing and love,
With life before and after
    And death beneath and above,
For a day and a night and a morrow,
    That his strength might endure for a span
With travail and heavy sorrow,
    The holy spirit of man. . . .

A. C. Swinburne

Our revels are now ended. These our actors,
As I foretold you, were all spirits and
Melted into air, into thin air:
And, like the baseless fabric of this vision,
The cloud-capp'd towers, the gorgeous palaces,
The solemn temples, the great globe itself,
Yea, all which it inherit, shall dissolve
And, like this insubstantial pageant faded,
Leave not a rack behind. We are such stuff
As dreams are made on, and our little life
Is rounded with a sleep.

William Shakespeare: *The Tempest*

HAMLET: To be, or not to be, that is the question:
Whether 'tis nobler in the mind to suffer
The slings and arrows of outrageous Fortune,
Or to take arms against a sea of troubles,
And by opposing end them: to die to sleep;
No more; and by a sleep, to say we end
The heart-ache, and the thousand natural shocks
That flesh is heir to; 'tis a consummation
Devoutly to be wish'd. To die to sleep,
To sleep, perchance to dream; ay, there's the rub,
For in that sleep of death, what dreams may come,
When we have shuffled off this mortal coil,
Must give us pause. There's the respect
That makes calamity of so long life:
For who would hear the whips and scorns of time,
The oppressor's wrong, the proud man's contumely,
The pangs of dispiz'd love, the Law's delay,

The insolence of office, and the spurns
That patient merit of the unworthy takes,
When he himself might his quietus make,
With a bare bodkin? who would fardels bear,
To grunt and sweat under a weary life,
But that the dread of something after death,
The undiscovered country, from whose bourn
No traveller returns, puzzles the will,
And makes us rather bear those ills we have,
Than fly to others that we know not of.

William Shakespeare: *Hamlet*

'Is not what we call death a freeing and separation of soul from body?'

'Certainly,' he said.

'And the desire to free the soul is found chiefly, or rather only, in the true philosopher; in fact the philosopher's occupation consists precisely in the freeing and separation of soul from body. Isn't that so?'

'Apparently.'

'Well then, as I said at the beginning, if a man has trained himself throughout his life to live in a state as close as possible to death, would it not be ridiculous for him to be distressed when death comes to him?'

'It would, of course.'

'Then it is a fact, Simmias, that true philosophers make dying their profession, and that to them of all men death is least alarming. Look at it in this way. If they are thoroughly dissatisfied with the body, and long to have their souls independent of it, when this happens would it not be entirely unreasonable to be frightened and distressed? Would they not naturally be glad to set out for the place where there is a prospect of attaining the object of their lifelong desire, which is Wisdom; and of escaping from an unwelcome association? Surely there are many who have chosen of their own free will to follow dead lovers and wives and sons to the next world, in the hope of seeing and meeting there the persons whom they loved. If this is so, will a true lover of wisdom who has firmly grasped this same conviction – that he will never attain to wisdom worthy of the name elsewhere than in the next world – will he be grieved at dying? Will he not be glad to make that journey? We must suppose so, my dear boy; that is, if he is a real philosopher; because then he will be of the firm belief that he will never find wisdom in all its purity in any other place. If this is so, would it not be quite unreasonable (as I said just now) for such a man to be afraid of death?'

'It would, indeed.'

Plato: *Phaedo*
translated H. Tredennick

All the World's a Stage

All the world's a stage,
    And all the men and women merely players:
They have their exits and their entrances;
    And one man in his time plays many parts,

His acts being seven ages. At first the infant,
    Mewling and puking in the nurse's arms.
And then the whining schoolboy, with his satchel,
    And shining morning face, creeping like snail
Unwillingly to school. And then the lover,
    Sighing like furnace, with a woeful ballad
Made to his mistress' eyebrow. Then a soldier,
    Full of strange oaths, and bearded like the pard,
Jealous in honour, sudden and quick in quarrel,
    Seeking the bubble reputation
Even in the cannon's mouth. And then the justice,
    In fair round belly with good capon lined,
With eyes severe and beard of formal cut,
    Full of wise saws and modern instances;
And so he plays his part. The sixth age shifts
    Into the lean and slippered pantaloon,
With spectacles on nose, and pouch on side;
    His youthful hose, well saved, a world too wide
For his shrunk shank; and his big manly voice,
    Turning again toward childish treble, pipes
And whistles in his sound. Last scene of all,
    That ends this strange eventful history,
Is second childishness and mere oblivion,
    Sans teeth, sans eyes, sans taste, sans everything.

William Shakespeare: *As You Like It*

All the World's a Stage

What is our life? A play of passion,
Our mirth the music of division.
Our mother's wombs the tiring-houses be,
Where we are dressed for this short comedy.
Heaven the judicious sharp spectator is,
That sits and marks still who doth act amiss.
Our graves that hide us from the searching sun
Are like drawn curtains when the play is done.
Thus march we, playing, to our latest rest.
Only we die in earnest, that's no jest.

Sir Walter Raleigh

Happy, O! happy he, who not affecting
The endless toils attending worldly cares,
With mind reposed, all discontents rejecting,
    In silent peace his way to heaven prepares,
Deeming this life a scene, the world a stage
Whereon man acts his weary pilgrimage.

From John Wilby's *Second Set of Madrigals*

Everyone Sang

Everyone suddenly burst out singing;
And I was filled with such delight
As prisoned birds must find in freedom,
Winging wildly across the white
Orchards and dark-green fields; on – on – and out of
    sight.

Everyone's voice was suddenly lifted;
And beauty came like the setting sun:
My heart was shaken with tears; and horror
Drifted away . . . O, but Everyone
Was a bird; and the song was wordless; the singing will
    never be done.

Siegfried Sassoon

The One Certainty

Vanity of vanities, the Preacher saith,
All things are vanity. The eye and ear
Cannot be filled with what they see and hear.
Like early dew, or like the sudden breath
Of wind, or like the grass that withereth,
Is man, tossed to and fro by hope and fear:
So little joy hath he, so little cheer,
Till all things end in the long dust of death.
To-day is still the same yesterday,

To-morrow also even as one of them;
And there is nothing new under the sun:
Until the ancient race of Time be run,
The old thorns shall grow out of the old stem,
And morning shall be cold and twilight grey.

Christina Rossetti

Youth in Age

Once I was part of the music I heard
On the boughs or sweet beneath earth and sky,
For joy of the beating of wings on high
My heart shot into the breast of the bird.

*   *   *

I hear it now and I see it fly,
And a life in wrinkles again is stirred,
My heart shoots into the breast of the bird,
As it will for sheer love till the last long sigh.

George Meredith

It is not growing like a tree
    In bulk, doth make Man better be;
    Or standing long an oak, three hundred year

To fall a log at last, dry, bald, and sere:
    A lily of a day
    Is fairer far in May,
  Although it fall and die that night;
  It was the plant and flower of Light.
In small proportions we just beauties see;
And in short measures life may perfect be.

Ben Jonson

It is over. What is over?
    Nay, how much is over truly! –
Harvest days we toiled to sow for;
    Now the sheaves are gathered newly,
    Now the wheat is garnered duly.

It is finished. What is finished?
    Much is finished known or unknown:
Lives are finished; time diminished;
    Was the fallow field left unsown?
    Will these buds be always unblown?

It suffices. What suffices?
    All suffices reckoned rightly:
Spring shall bloom where now the ice is,
    Roses make the bramble sightly,
    And the quickening sun shine brightly,
    And the latter wind blow lightly,
And my garden teem with spices.

Christina Rossetti

Days

What are days for?
Days are where we live.
They come, they wake us
Time and time over.
They are to be happy in:
Where can we live but days?

Ah, solving that question
Brings the priest and the doctor
In their long coats
Running over the fields.

Philip Larkin

Man's life is well comparëd to a feast,
Furnished with choice of all variety:
To it comes Time; and as a bidden guest
He sets him down, in pomp and majesty;
The three-fold age of man, the waiters be;
  Then with an earthen voider (made of clay)
  Comes Death, and takes the table clean away.

Richard Barnfield

The World a Hunt

The World a-hunting is:
The prey poor Man, the Nimrod fierce is Death;
His speedy greyhounds are
Lust, Sickness, Envy, Care,
Strife that ne'er falls amiss,
With all those ills which haunt us while we breathe.
Now if by chance we fly
Of these the eager chase,
Old Age with stealing pace
Casts up his nets, and there we panting die.

                    William Drummond of Hawthornden

'Tis true our life is but a long dis-ease,
Made up of real pain and seeming ease.
You stars, whose entangled fortunes give,
    O tell me why
    It is so hard to die,
        Yet such a task to live?

If with some pleasure we our griefs betray,
It costs us dearer than it can repay.
For time or fortune all things so devours;
    Our hopes are crost,
    Or else the object lost,
        'Ere we can call it ours.

                            Katherine Philips

Life Ephemeral

We come only to sleep, we come only to dream,
It is not true, it is not true that we come to live on earth.

We come to be transformed into the spring grasses,
Our hearts come here to put on fresh green. They come
   here to open their petals.

Our body is a flower, it gives birth to flowers, and it
   withers.

Anonymous Nahuatl Poem
(Adapted from a Spanish version by J. M. Cohen)

From The Book of Job

Man that is born of a woman is of few
days, and full of trouble.
   He cometh forth like a flower, and is cut
down: he fleeth also as a shadow, and continueth not.
   And dost thou open thine eyes upon such
an one, and bringest me into judgment with thee?
   Who can bring a clean thing out of an
unclean? not one.
   Seeing his days are determined, the
number of his months are with thee, thou
hast appointed his bounds that he cannot
pass;

Turn from him, that he may rest, till he
shall accomplish, as an hireling, his day.

For there is hope of a tree, if it be cut
down, that it will sprout again, and that the
tender branch thereof will not cease.

Though the root thereof wax old in the
earth, and the stock thereof die in the ground;

Yet through the scent of water it will bud,
and bring forth boughs like a plant.

But man dieth, and wasteth away: yea,
man giveth up the ghost, and where is he?

As the waters fail from the sea, and the
flood decayeth and drieth up:

So man lieth down, and riseth not: till
the heavens be no more, they shall not
awake, nor be raised out of their sleep.

Chapter 14:1–12

No young man believes he shall ever die. It was a saying
of my brother's, and a fine one. There is a feeling of
Eternity in youth which makes us amends for everything.
To be young is to be as one of the Immortals. One half
of time indeed is spent – the other half remains in store
for us with all its countless treasures, for there is no line
drawn, and we see no limit to our hopes and wishes. We
make the coming age our own –

'The vast, the unbounded prospect lies before us.'

Death, old age, are words without a meaning, a dream, a
fiction, with which we have nothing to do. Others may
have undergone, or may still undergo them – we 'bear a
charmed life,' which laughs to scorn all such idle fancies.
As, in setting out on a delightful journey, we strain our
eager sight forward.

> 'Bidding the lovely scenes at distance hail,'

and see no end to prospect after prospect, new objects
presenting themselves as we advance, so in the outset of
life we see no end to our desires nor to the opportunities
of gratifying them. We have as yet found no obstacle, no
disposition to flag, and it seems that we can go on so for
ever. We look round in a new world, full of life and
motion, and ceaseless progress, and feel in ourselves all
the vigour and spirit to keep pace with it, and do not
foresee from any present signs how we shall be left
behind in the race, decline into old age, and drop into
the grave. It is the simplicity and, as it were, abstractedness
of our feelings in youth that (so to speak) identifies us
with Nature and (our experience being weak and our
passions strong) makes us fancy ourselves immortal like
it. Our short-lived connexion with being, we fondly
flatter ourselves, is an indissoluble and lasting union. As
infants smile and sleep, we are rocked in the cradle of
our desires, and hushed into fancied security by the roar
of the universe around us – we quaff the cup of life with
eager thirst without draining it, and joy and hope seem
ever mantling to the brim – objects press around us,
filling the mind with their magnitude and with the
throng of desires that wait upon them, so that there is no
room for the thoughts of death.

William Hazlitt: from *On the Feeling of Immortality in Youth*

Some say that gleams of a remoter world
Visit the soul in sleep, – that death is slumber,
And that its shapes the busy thoughts outnumber
Of those who wake and live. – I look on high;
Has some unknown omnipotence unfurled
The veil of life and death? or do I lie
In dream, and does the mightier world of sleep
Spread far around and inaccessibly
Its circles? For the very spirits fails,
Driven like a homeless cloud from steep to steep
That vanishes among the viewless gales!
Far, far above, piercing the infinite sky,
Mont Blanc appears, – still, snowy, and serene –
Its subject mountains their unearthly forms
Pile around it, ice and rock; broad vales between
Of frozen floods, unfathomable deeps,
Blue as the overhanging heaven, that spread
And wind among the accumulated steeps;
A desert peopled by the storms alone,
Save when the eagle brings some hunter's bone,
And the wolf tracks her there – how hideously
Its shapes are heaped around! rude, bare, and high,
Ghastly, and scarred, and riven. – Is this the scene
Where the old Earthquake-daemon taught her young
Ruin? Were these their toys? or did a sea
Of fire envelop once this silent snow?
None can reply – all seems eternal now.
The wilderness has a mysterious tongue
Which teaches awful doubt, or faith so mild,
So solemn, so serene, that man may be,
But for such faith, with nature reconciled;
Thou has a voice, great Mountain, to repeal
Large codes of fraud and woe; not understood
By all, but which the wise, and great, and good
Interpret, or make felt, or deeply feel.

                         P. B. Shelley: from *Mont Blanc*

But often, in the world's most crowded streets,
But often, in the din of strife,
There rises an unspeakable desire
After the knowledge of our buried life;
A thirst to spend our fire and restless force
In tracking out our true, original course;
A longing to inquire
Into the mystery of this heart which beats
So wild, so deep in us – to know
Whence our lives come and where they go.
And many a man in his own breast then delves,
But deep enough, alas! none ever mines.
And we have been on many thousand lines,
And we have shown, on each, spirit and power;
But hardly have we, for one little hour,
Been on our own line, have we been ourselves –
Hardly had skill to utter one of all
The nameless feelings that course through our breast,
But they course on for ever unexpress'd.
And long we try in vain to speak and act
Our hidden self, and what we say and do
Is eloquent, is well – but 'tis not true!
And then we will no more be rack'd
With inward striving, and demand
Of all the thousand nothings of the hour
Their stupefying power;
Ah yes, and they benumb us at our call!
Yet still, from time to time, vague and forlorn,
From the soul's subterranean depth upborne
As from an infinitely distant land,
Come airs, and floating echoes, and convey
A melancholy into all our day.

Only – but this is rare –
When a belovéd hand is laid in ours.
When, jaded with the rush and glare
Of the interminable hours,
Our eyes can in another's eyes read clear,
When our world-deafen'd ear
Is by the tones of a loved voice caress'd –
A bolt is shot back somewhere in our breast,
And a lost pulse of feeling stirs again.
The eye sinks inward, and the heart lies plain,
And what we mean, we say, and what we would, we
    know
A man becomes aware of his life's flow,
And hears its winding murmur; and he sees
The meadows where it glides, the sun, the breeze.

And there arrives a lull in the hot race
Wherein he doth for ever chase
That flying and elusive shadow, rest.
An air of coolness plays upon his face,
And an unwonted calm pervades his breast
And then he thinks he knows
The hills where his life rose,
And the sea where it goes.

Matthew Arnold: from *The Buried Life*

Man's Days

A sudden wakin', a sudden weepin';
A li'l suckin', a li'l sleepin';
A cheel's full joys an' a cheel's short sorrows,
Wi' a power o' faith in gert to-morrows.

Young blood red hot an' the love of a maid;
Wan glorious hour as'll never fade;
Some shadows, some sunshine, some triumphs, some
   tears;
An' a gatherin' weight o' the flyin' years.

Then auld man's talk o' the days behind 'e;
Your darter's youngest darter to mind 'e;
A li'l dreamin', a li'l dyin',
A li'l lew corner o' airth to lie in.

                                        Eden Phillpotts

Afterwards

When the Present has latched its postern behind my
      tremulous stay,
   And the May month flaps its glad green leaves like
      wings,
Delicate-filmed as new-spun silk, will the neighbours
      say,
   'He was a man who used to notice such things'?

If it be in the dusk when, like an eyelid's soundless blink,
    The dewfall-hawk comes crossing the shades to alight
Upon the wind-warped upland thorn, a gazer may
        think,
    'To him this must have been a familiar sight.'

If I pass during some nocturnal blackness, mothy and
        warm,
    When the hedgehog travels furtively over the lawn,
One may say, 'He strove that such innocent creatures
        should come to no harm,
    But he could do little for them; and now he is gone.'

If, when hearing that I have been stilled at last, they
        stand at the door,
    Watching the full-starred heavens that winter sees,
Will this thought rise on those who will meet my face
        no more,
    'He was one who had an eye for such mysteries'?

And will any say when my bell of quittance is heard in
        the gloom,
    And a crossing breeze cuts a pause in its outrollings,
Till they rise again, as they were a new bell's boom,
    'He hears it not now, but used to notice such things'?

                                        Thomas Hardy

The Mystery of Life

So many years I've seen the sun,
    And called these eyes and hands my own,
A thousand little acts I've done,
    And childhood have and manhood known:
O what is life? and this dull round
To tread, why was a spirit bound?

So many airy draughts and lines,
    And warm excursions of the mind,
Have filled my soul with great designs,
    While practice grovelled far behind:
O what is thought? and where withdraw
The glories which my fancy saw?

So many tender joys and woes
    Have on my quivering soul had power;
Plain life with height'ning passions rose,
    The boast or burden of their hour:
O what is all we feel? why fled
Those pains and pleasures o'er my head?

So many human souls divine,
    So at one interview displayed,
Some oft and freely mixed with mine,
    In lasting bonds my heart have laid:
O what is friendship? why impressed
On my weak, wretched, dying breast?

So many wondrous gleams of light,
   And gentle ardours from above,
Have made me sit, like seraph bright,
   Some moments on a throne of love:
O what is virtue? why had I,
Who am so low, a taste so high?

Ere long, when sovereign Wisdom wills,
   My soul an unknown path shall tread,
And strangely leave, who strangely fills
   This frame, and waft me to the dead.

O what is death? 'tis life's last shore,
Where vanities are vain no more;
Where all pursuits their goal obtain,
And life is all retouched again;
Where in their bright result shall rise
Thoughts, virtues, friendships, griefs and joys.

                    John Gambold

This Life

    This Life, which seems so fair,
Is like a bubble blown up in the air
      By sporting children's breath,
    Who chase it everywhere,
And strive who can most motion it bequeath.
And though it sometimes seem of its own might
Like to an eye of gold to be fixed there,

And firm to hover in that empty height,
That only is because it is so light.
    But in that pomp it doth not long appear;
For when 'tis most admirèd – in a thought,
Because it erst was nought, it turns to nought.

                          William Drummond of Hawthornden

Change Should Breed Change

New doth the sun appear,
The mountains' snows decay,
Crowned with frail flowers forth comes the baby year.
My soul, time posts away,
And thou yet in that frost
Which flower and fruit hath lost,
As if all here immortal were, dost stay:
For shame! thy powers awake,
Look to that heaven which never night makes black,
And there, at that immortal sun's bright rays,
Deck thee with flowers which fear not rage of days.

                          William Drummond of Hawthornden

Echo's Lament for Narcissus

Slow, slow, fresh fount, keep time with my salt tears;
　　Yet, slower yet; O faintly, gentle springs;
List to the heavy part the music bears;
　　Woe weeps out her division when she sings.
　　　　Droop herbs and flowers;
　　　　Fall grief in showers,
　　　　Our beauties are not ours;
　　　　　O, I could still,
Like melting snow upon some craggy hill,
　　　　Drop, drop, drop, drop,
Since nature's pride is now a withered daffodil.

Ben Jonson

Hawthorn had lost his motley livery,
The naked twigs were shivering all for cold,
And dropping down the tears abundantly;
Each thing, methought, with weeping eye me told
The cruel season, bidding me withhold
　　Myself within; for I was gotten out
　　Into the fields, whereas I walk'd about.

*　　　*　　　*

And sorrowing I to see the summer flowers,
The lively green, the lusty leas forlorn,
The sturdy trees so shatter'd with the showers,
The fields so fade that flourish'd so beforn,
It taught me well, all earthly things be born
    To die the death, for nought long time may last
    The summer's beauty yields to winter's blast.

Thomas Sackville, Lord Buckhurst

Sic Vita

    Like to the falling of a star,
Or as the flights of eagles are,
Or like the fresh spring's gaudy hue,
Or silver drops of morning dew,
Or like a wind that chafes the flood,
Or bubbles which on water stood:
Even such is man, whose borrowed light
Is straight called in, and paid to night.

The wind blows out, the bubble dies;
The spring entombed in autumn lies;
The dew dries up, the star is shot;
The flight is past: and man forgot.

Henry King

To their long home the greatest princes go
    In hearses dressed with fair escutcheons round,
    The blazons of an ancient race, renowned
For deeds of valour; and in costly show
The train moves forward in procession slow
    Towards some hallowed fane; no common ground,
    But the arched vault and tomb with sculpture
      crowned
Receive the corpse, with honours laid below.
    Alas! whate'er their wealth, their wit, their worth,
    Such is the end of all the sons of earth.

Sir John Beaumont: *Upon a Funeral. Bosworth Field*

Death is before me to-day,
Like the recovery of a sick man,
Like going forth into a garden after sickness;
Death is before me to-day,
Like the odour of myrrh,
– Like sitting under the sail on a windy day;
Death is before me to-day,
Like the odour of lotus flowers,
Like sitting on the shore of drunkeness;
Death is before me to-day,
Like the course of the freshet,
Like the return of a man from the war-galley to his
    house,
When he has spent years in captivity.

Anon. *Egyptian Poem*

Mutability

We are as clouds that veil the midnight moon;
    How restlessly they speed, and gleam, and quiver,
Streaking the darkness radiantly! – yet soon
    Night closes round, and they are lost for ever:

Or like forgotten lyres, whose dissonant strings
    Give various response to each varying blast,
To whose frail frame no second motion brings
    One mood or modulation like the last.

We rest. – A dream has power to poison sleep;
    We rise. – One wandering thought pollutes the day
We feel, conceive or reason, laugh or weep;
    Embrace fond woe, or cast our cares away:

It is the same! – For, be it joy or sorrow,
    The path of its departure still is free:
Man's yesterday may ne'er be like his morrow;
    Nought may endure but Mutability.

P. B. Shelley

Death the Leveller

The glories of our blood and state
    Are shadows, not substantial things;
There is no armour against Fate;
    Death lays his icy hand on kings:
        Sceptre and Crown
        Must tumble down,
And in the dust be equal made
With the poor crooked scythe and spade.

Some men with swords may reap the field,
    And plant fresh laurels where they kill:
But their strong nerves at last must yield;
    They tame but one another still:
        Early or late
        They stoop to fate,
And must give up their murmuring breath
When they, pale captives, creep to death.

The garlands wither on your brow;
    Then boast no more your mighty deeds!
Upon Death's purple altar now
    See where the victor-victim bleeds.
        Your heads must come
        To the cold tomb:
Only the actions of the just
Smell sweet and blossom in their dust.

James Shirley

. . . For I have learned
To look on nature, not as in the hour
Of thoughtless youth; but hearing oftentimes
The still, sad music of humanity,
Nor harsh nor grating, though of ample power
To chasten and subdue. And I have felt
A presence that disturbs me with the joy
Of elevated thoughts; a sense sublime
Of something far more deeply interfused,
Whose dwelling is the light of setting suns,
And the round ocean and the living air,
And the blue sky, and in the mind of man:
A motion and a spirit, that impels
All thinking things, all objects of all thought,
And rolls through all things. Therefore am I still
A lover of the meadows and the woods,
And mountains; and of all that we behold
From this green earth; of all the mighty world
Of eye, and ear, – both what they half create,
And what perceive; well pleased to recognise
In nature and the language of the sense
The anchor of my purest thoughts, the nurse,
The guide, the guardian of my heart, and soul
Of all my moral being.

                    William Wordsworth: from *Tintern Abbey*

Valediction to the River Duddon

I thought of Thee, my partner and my guide,
    As being past away. – Vain sympathies!
    For, backward, Duddon! as I cast my eyes,
I see what was, and is, and will abide;
Still glides the Stream, and shall for ever glide;
    The Form remains, the Function never dies;
    While we, the brave, the mighty, and the wise,
We Men, who in our morn of youth defied
The elements, must vanish; – be it so!
    Enough, if something from our hands have power
    To live, and act, and serve the future hour;
And if, as toward the silent tomb we go,
    Through love, through hope, and faith's transcendent
        dower,
We feel that we are greater than we know.

                        William Wordsworth

    A slumber did my spirit seal;
        I had no human fears:
    She seemed a thing that could not feel
        The touch of earthly years.

    No motion has she now, no force;
        She neither hears nor sees;
    Rolled round in earth's diurnal course,
        With rocks, and stones, and trees.

                        William Wordsworth

I am: yet what I am none cares or knows,
    My friends forsake me like a memory lost;
I am the self-consumer of my woes,
    They rise and vanish in oblivious host,
Like shades in love and death's oblivion lost;
And yet I am, and live with shadows tost.

Into the nothingness of scorn and noise,
    Into the living sea of waking dreams,
Where there is neither sense of life nor joys,
    But the vast shipwreck of my life's esteems;
And een the dearest – that I loved the best –
Are strange – nay, rather stranger than the rest.

I long for scenes where man has never trod;
    A place where woman never smiled or wept;
There to abide with my Creator, God,
    And sleep as I in childhood sweetly slept;
Untroubling and untroubled where I lie;
The grass below – above the vaulted sky.

                                        John Clare

2

Love and Death

Spring and Fall
to a Young Child

Márgarét, áre you gríeving
Over Goldengrove unleaving?
Léaves, líke the things of man, you
With your fresh thoughts care for, can you!
Áh! ás the heart grows older
It will come to such sights colder
By and by, nor spare a sigh
Though worlds of wanwood leafmeal lie,
And yet you *will* weep and know why.
Now no matter, child, the name:
Sórrow's spríngs áre the same.
Nor mouth had, no nor mind, expressed
What heart heard of, ghost guessed:
It ís the blight man was born for,
It is Margaret you mourn for.

Gerard Manley Hopkins

The Burning of the Leaves

Now is the time for the burning of the leaves.
They go to the fire; the nostril pricks with smoke
Wandering slowly into a weeping mist.
Brittle and blotched, ragged and rotten sheaves!
A flame seizes the smouldering ruin and bites
On stubborn stalks that crackle as they resist.

The last hollyhock's fallen tower is dust;
All the spices of June are a bitter reek,
All the extravagent riches spent and mean.
All burns! the reddest rose is a ghost;
Sparks whirl up, to expire in the mist: the wild
Fingers of fire are making corruption clean.

Now is the time for stripping the spirit bare,
Time for the burning of days ended and done,
Idle solace of things that have gone before:
Rootless hope and fruitless desire are there;
Let them go to the fire, with never a look behind.
The world that was ours is a world that is ours no more.

They will come again, the leaf and the flower, to arise
From squalor of rottenness into the old splendour,
And magical scents to a wondering memory bring;
The same glory, to shine upon different eyes.
Earth cares for her own ruins, naught for ours.
Nothing is certain, only the certain spring.

                                                    Laurence Binyon

Tired with all these, for restful death I cry;
    As to behold desert a beggar born,
And needy nothing trimmed in jollity,
    And purest faith unhappily forsworn,
And gilded honour shamefully misplaced,
    And maiden virtue rudely strumpeted,
And right perfection wrongfully disgraced,
    And strength by limping sway disabled,
And art made tongue-tied by authority,
    And folly, doctor-like, controlling skill,
And simple truth miscalled simplicity,
    And captive good attending captain ill.
      Tired with all these, from these would I be gone,
      Save that, to die, I leave my Love alone.

                        William Shakespeare

Memories of President Lincoln
When Lilacs Last In The Dooryard Bloom'd

I

When lilacs last in the dooryard bloom'd,
And the great star early droop'd in the western sky in
    the night,
I mourn'd, and yet shall mourn with ever-returning
    spring.

Ever-returning spring, trinity sure to me you bring,
Lilac blooming perennial and drooping star in the west,
And thought of him I love.

                        Walt Whitman

... But true love is a durable fire,
   In the mind ever burning,
Never sick, never dead, never cold,
   From itself never turning.

Sir Walter Raleigh

Alcuin Writes to His Friend,
Arno of Salzburg, Many Leagues Away

No mountain and no forest, land nor sea,
Shall block love's road, deny the way to thee ...
Yet why must love that's sweet
So bitter tears beget,
Honey and gall in one same goblet set?
Even so, O world, the feet
Of sorrow follow hard upon delight,
Joy breaketh in a cry,
And all sweet things are changed to bitterness.
They will not stay for me: yea, all things haste to die.

Wherefore, O world,
So soon to die,
From us depart,
And thou, my heart,
Make haste to fly
Where is delight that fades not,
The unchanging shore,
The happy house where friend from friend divides not,

And what he loves, he hath for ever more.
Take me, beloved, in thy prayer with thee,
Where shall be no estranging thee and me.

From *Poetry in the Dark Ages*
(A lecture delivered by Helen Waddell)

Shang Ya!
I want to be your friend
For ever and ever without break or decay.
When the hills are all flat
And the rivers are all dry,
When it lightens and thunders in winter,
When it rains and snows in summer,
When Heaven and Earth mingle –
Not till then will I part from you.

Translated by Arthur Waley: *Chinese Oaths of Friendship*

My dearest consort, my more loved heart,
I leave thee now; with thee all earthly joying,
Heaven knows with thee alone I sadly part:
All other earthly sweets have had their cloying;
    Yet never full of thy sweet love's enjoying,
Thy constant loves, next Heaven, I did refer them:
Had not much grave prevail'd, 'for Heav'n I should
        prefer them.

I leave them, now the trumpet calls away;
In vain thine eyes beg for some time's reprieving;
Yet in my children here immortal stay;
In one I die, in many ones am living:
   In them, and for them, stay thy too much grieving:
Look but on them, in them thou still wilt see
Married with thee again thy twice-two Antony.

   And when with little hands, they stroke thy face,
As in thy lap they sit (ah, careless!) playing,
And stammering ask a kiss, give them a brace;
The last from me: and then a little staying,
And in their face some part of me surveying,
In them give me a third and with a tear
Show thy dear love to him, who loved thee ever dear....

... Farewell, Farewell! I feel my long, long rest,
And iron sleep, my leaden heart oppressing:
Night after day, sleep after labour's best;
Port after storms, joy after long distressing;
   So weep thy loss, as knowing 'tis my blessing:
Both as a widow and a Christian grieve:
Still live I in thy thoughts, but as in Heaven I live.

Phineas Fletcher: from *The Dying Husband's Farewell*

When you and I go down
Breathless and cold,
Our faces both worn back
To earthly mould,
How lonely we shall be!
What shall we do,
You without me,
I without you?

I cannot bear the thought
You, first, may die,
Nor of how you will weep,
Should I.
We are too much alone;
What can we do
To make our bodies one;
You, me, I, you? . . .
Is then nothing safe?
Can we not find
Some everlasting life
In our one mind?
I feel it like disgrace
Only to understand
Your spirit through your word,
Or by your hand.
I cannot find a way
Through love and through;
I cannot reach beyond
Body, to you.
When you or I must go
Down evermore,
There'll be no more to say
– But a locked door.

Harold Monro: from *Midlight Lamentation*

Breathless, we flung us on the windy hill,
    Laughed in the sun, and kissed the lovely grass.
    You said, 'Through glory and ecstasy we pass;
Wind, sun, and earth remain, the birds sing still,
When we are old, are old. . . .' 'And when we die
    All's over that is ours; and life burns on
Through other lovers, other lips,' said I,
    'Heart of my heart, our heaven is now, is won!'

'We are Earth's best, that learnt her lesson here.
    Life is our cry. We have kept the faith!' we said;
    'We shall go down with unreluctant tread
Rose-crowned into the darkness!' . . . Proud we were,
And laughed, that had such brave true things to say.
– And then you suddenly cried, and turned away.

                                                        Rupert Brooke

When our two souls stand up erect and strong,
    Face to face, silent, drawing nigh and nigher,
    Until the lengthening wings break into fire
At either curvèd point, – what bitter wrong
Can the earth do to us, that we should not long
    Be here contented? Think! In mounting higher,
    The angels would press on us, and aspire
To drop some golden orb of perfect song
Into our deep, dear silence. Let us stay
    Rather on earth, Beloved – where the unfit

Contrarious moods of men recoil away
   And isolate pure spirits, and permit
A place to stand and love in for a day,
   With darkness and the death-hour rounding it.

Elizabeth Barrett Browning

The Great Lover

I have been so great a lover: filled my days
So proudly with the splendour of Love's praise,
The pain, the calm, and the astonishment,
Desire illimitable, and still content,
And all dear names men use, to cheat despair,
For the perplexed and viewless streams that bear
Our hearts at random down the dark of life.
Now, ere the unthinking silence on that strife
Steals down, I would cheat drowsy Death so far,
My night shall be remembered for a star
That outshone all the suns of all men's days.
Shall I not crown them with immortal praise
Whom I have loved, who have given me, dared with
     me
High secrets, and in darkness knelt to see
The inenarrable godhead of delight?
Love is a flame; – we have beaconed the world's night.
A city: – and we have built it, these and I.
An emperor: – we have taught the world to die.
So, for their sakes I loved, ere I go hence,
And the high cause of Love's magnificence,

And to keep loyalties young, I'll write those names
Golden for ever, eagles, crying flames,
And set them as a banner, that men may know,
To dare the generations, burn, and blow
Out on the wind of Time, shining and streaming . . .

These I have loved:
            White plates and cups, clean-gleaming,
Ringed with blue lines; and feathery, faery dust;
Wet roofs, beneath the lamp-light; the strong crust
Of friendly bread; and many-tasting food;
Rainbows; and the blue bitter smoke of wood;
And radiant raindrops couching in cool flowers;
And flowers themselves, that sway through sunny
      hours,
Dreaming of moths that drink them under the moon;
Then, the cool kindliness of sheets, that soon
Smooth away trouble; and the rough male kiss
Of blankets; grainy wood; live hair that is
Shining and free; blue-massing clouds; the keen
Unpassioned beauty of a great machine;
The benison of hot water; furs to touch;
The good smell of old clothes; and other such –
The comfortable smell of friendly fingers,
Hair's fragrance, and the musty reek that lingers
About dead leaves and last year's ferns . . .
                                    Dear names,
And thousand other throng to me! Royal flames;
Sweet water's dimpling laugh from tap or spring;
Holes in the ground; and voices that do sing;
Voices in laughter, too; and body's pain,
Soon turned to peace; and the deep-panting train;
Firm sands; the little dulling edge of foam
That browns and dwindles as the wave goes home;

And washen stones, gay for an hour; the cold
Graveness of iron; moist black earthen mould;
Sleep; and high places; footprints in the dew;
And oaks; and brown horse-chestnuts, glossy-new;
And new-peeled sticks; and shining pools on grass; –
All these have been my loves. And these shall pass,
Whatever passes not, in the great hour,
Nor all my passion, all my prayers, have power
To hold them with me through the gate of Death.
They'll play deserter, turn with the traitor breath,
Break the high bond we made, and sell Love's trust
And sacramented covenant to the dust.
– Oh, never a doubt but, somewhere, I shall wake,
And give what's left of love again, and make
New friends, now strangers . . .
                But the best I've known,
Stays here, and changes, breaks, grows old, is blown
About the winds of the world, and fades from brains
Of living men, and dies.
                Nothing remains.
O dear my loves, O faithless, once again
This one last gift I give: that after men
Shall know, and later lovers, far-removed,
Praise you, 'All these were lovely'; say, 'He loved.'

                         Rupert Brooke

'Yes, love (he thought again with perfect distinctness),
but not that love that loves for something, to gain
something, or because of something, but that love that I
felt for the first time, when dying, I saw my enemy and
yet loved him. I knew that feeling of love which is the
very essence of the soul, for which no object is needed.
And I know that blissful feeling now too. To love one's
neighbours, to love one's enemies. To love everything –
to love God in all His manifestations. Someone dear to
one can be loved with human love; but an enemy can
only be loved with divine love. And that was why I felt
such joy when I felt I loved that man. What happened to
him? Is he alive? . . . Loving with human love, one may
pass from love to hatred; but divine love cannot change.
Nothing, not even death, can shatter it. It is the very
nature of the soul . . .

'Love is life. All, all that I understand, I understand
only because I love. All is, all exists only because I love.
All is bound up in love alone. Love is God, and dying
means for me a particle of love, to go back to the
universal and eternal source of love'.

From Tolstoy's *War and Peace*
Translated by Constance Garnett

3

Fear of Death

Men fear death, as children fear to go in the dark; and as that natural fear in children is increased with tales, so is the other. Certainly, the contemplation of death, as the *wages of sin,* and passage to another world, is holy and religious; but the fear of it, as a tribute due unto nature, is weak. Yet in religious meditations there is sometimes mixture of vanity and of superstition. You shall read in some of the friars' books of mortification, that a man should think with himself what the pain is if he have but his finger's end pressed or tortured, and thereby imagine what the pains of death are, when the whole body is corrupted and dissolved: when many times death passeth with less pain than the torture of a limb; for the most vital parts are not the quickest of sense. . . .

Francis Bacon: *Essay – Of Death*

. . . It is as natural to die as to be born; and to a little infant, perhaps, the one is as painful as the other. He that dies in an earnest pursuit is like one that is wounded in hot blood; who, for the time, scarce feels the hurt; and therefore a mind fixed and bent upon somewhat that is good doth avert the dolours of death. But above all, believe it, the sweetest canticle is *Nunc dimittis*; when a man hath obtained worthy ends and expectations. Death hath this also, that it openeth the gate to good frame, and extinguisheth envy.

Francis Bacon: *Essay – Of Death*

Since Nature's workes be good, and death doth serve
As Nature's worke, why should we feare to die?
Since feare is vaine but when it may preserve,
Why should we feare that which we cannot flie?
Feare is more paine than is the paine it feares,
Disarming humane mindes of native might;
While each conceit an ougly figure beares,
Which were not evill, well view'd in reason's light.
Our only eyes, which dimm'd with passions be,
And scarce discerne the dawne of comming day,
Let them be clear'd, and now begin to see
Our life is but a step in dustie way:
Then let us hold the blisse of peacefull minde,
Since this we feele, great losse we cannot finde.

Sir Philip Sidney

No young man ever thinks he shall die. He may believe
that others will, or assent to the doctrine that 'all men are
mortal' as an abstract proposition, but he is far enough
from bringing it home to himself individually. Youth,
buoyant activity, and animal spirits, hold absolute
antipathy with old age as well as with death; nor have
we, in the hey-day of life, any more than in the
thoughtlessness of childhood, the remotest conception
how

> 'This sensible warm motion can become
> A kneaded clod' –

nor how sanguine, florid health and vigour, shall 'turn
to withered, weak, and grey.' Or if in a moment of idle
speculation we indulge in this notion of the close of life
as a theory, it is amazing at what a distance it seems;
what a long, leisurely interval there is between; what a
contrast its slow and solemn approach affords to our
present gay dreams of existence! We eye the farthest
verge of the horizon, and think what a way we shall
have to look back upon, ere we arrive at our journey's
end; and without our in the least suspecting it, the mists
are at our feet, and the shadows of age encompass us. The
two divisions of our lives have melted into each other:
the extreme points close and meet with none of that
romantic interval stretching out between them that we
had reckoned upon; and for the rich, melancholy, solemn
hues of age, 'the sear, the yellow leaf,' the deepening
shadows of an autumnal evening, we only feel a dank,
cold mist, encircling all objects, after the spirit of youth
is fled. There is no inducement to look forward; and
what is worse, little interest in looking back to what has
become so trite and common. The pleasures of our
existence have worn themselves out, are 'gone into the
wastes of time,' or have turned their indifferent side to

us: the pains by their repeated blows have worn us out, and have left us neither spirit nor inclination to encounter them again in retrospect. We do not want to rip up old grievances, nor to renew our youth like the phœnix, nor to live our lives twice over. Once is enough. As the tree falls, so let it lie. Shut up the book and close the account once for all!

William Hazlitt: from *On the Fear of Death*

Death and departure of friends are things generally grievous, the most austere and bitter accidents that can happen to a man in this life, to part for ever, to forsake the world and all our friends, 'tis the last and the greatest terror, most irksome and troublesome to us. And though we hope for a better life, eternal happiness, after these painful and miserable days, yet we cannot compose ourselves willingly to die; the remembrance of it is most grievious unto us, especially to such who are fortunate and rich; they start at the name of death, as a horse at a rotten post. . . .

Robert Burton: from *Anatomy of Melancholy*

It has been thought by some that life is like the exploration of a passage that grows narrower and darker the farther we advance, without a possibility of ever turning back, and where we are stifled for want of breath at last. For myself, I do not complain of the greater thickness of the atmosphere as I approach the narrow house. I felt it more formerly, when the idea alone seemed to suppress a thousand rising hopes, and weighed upon the pulses of the blood. At present I rather feel a thinness and want of support, I stretch out my hand to some object and find none, I am too much in a world of abstraction; the naked map of life is spread out before me, and in the emptiness and desolation I see Death coming to meet me. In my youth I could not behold him for the crowd of objects and feelings, and Hope stood always between us, saying, 'Never mind that old fellow!' If I had lived indeed, I should not care to die. But I do not like a contract of pleasure broken off unfulfilled, a marriage with joy unconsummated, a promise of happiness rescinded. My public and private hopes have been left a ruin, or remain only to mock me. I would wish them to be re-edified. I should like to see some prospect of good to mankind, such as my life began with. I should like to leave some sterling work behind me. I should like to have some friendly hand to consign me to the grave. On these conditions I am ready, if not willing, to depart. I shall then write on my tomb – GRATEFUL AND CONTENTED!

William Hazlitt: from *On the Fear of Death*

To die is only to be as we were before we were born;
yet no one feels any remorse, or regret, or repugnance,
in contemplating this last idea. It is rather a relief and
disburthening of the mind; it seems to have been holiday-
time with us then; we were not called to appear upon
the stage of life, to wear robes or tatters, to laugh or cry,
be hooted or applauded; we had lain *perdus* all this while,
snug, out of harm's way; and had slept out our thousands
of centuries without wanting to be waked up; at peace
and free from care, in a long nonage, in a sleep deeper
and calmer than that of infancy, wrapped in the softest
and finest dust. And the worst that we dread is, after a
short, fretful, feverish being, after vain hopes and idle
fears, to sink to final repose again, and forget the troubled
dream of life. . . .

William Hazlitt: from *On the Fear of Death*

O yet we trust that somehow good
Will be the final goal of ill,
To pangs of nature, sins of will
Defects of doubt, and taints of blood;

That nothing walks with aimless feet;
  That not one life shall be destroy'd
    Or cast as rubbish to the void;
When God hath made the pile complete; . . .

... Behold we know not anything;
    I can but trust that good shall fall
At last – far off – at last, to all.
And every winter change to spring.

So runs my dream: but what am I?
An infant crying in the night:
An infant crying for the light:
And with no language but a cry. . . .

... I falter where I firmly trod,
    And falling with my weight of cares
Upon the great world's altar stairs
That slope through darkness up to God,

I stretch lame hands of faith, and grope,
And gather dust and chaff, and call
To what I feel is Lord of all,
And faintly trust the larger hope.

Alfred, Lord Tennyson: from *In Memoriam*

Aye, but to die, and go we know not where;
To lie in cold obstruction and to rot;
This sensible warm motion to become
A kneaded clod; and the delighted spirit
To bathe in fiery floods, or to reside
In thrilling region of thick-ribbed ice;
To be imprison'd in the viewless winds,
And blown with restless violence round about

The pendant world; or to be worse than worst
Of those that lawless and incertain thoughts
Imagine howling: 'tis too horrible!
The weariest and most loathed worldly life
That age, ache, penury and imprisonment
Can lay on nature is a paradise
To what we fear of death.

William Shakespeare: *Measure for Measure*

Prospice

Fear death? – to feel the fog in my throat,
    The mist in my face,
When the snows begin, and the blasts denote
    I am nearing the place,
The power of the night, the press of the storm,
    The post of the foe;
Where he stands, the Arch Fear in a visible form,
    Yet the strong man must go:
For the journey is done and the summit attained,
    And the barriers fall,
Though a battle's to fight ere the guerdon be gained,
    The reward of it all.
I was ever a fighter, so – one fight more,
    The best and the last!
I would hate that death bandaged my eyes, and
        forebore,
    And bade me creep past.

No! let me taste the whole of it, fare like my peers
    The heroes of old,
Bear the brunt, in a minute pay glad life's arrears
    Of pain, darkness and cold.
For sudden the worst turns the best to the brave,
    The black minute's at end,
And the element's rage, the fiend-voices that rave,
    Shall dwindle, shall blend,
Shall challenge, shall become first a peace, then a joy,
    Then a light, then thy breast,
O thou soul of my soul! I shall clasp thee again,
    And with God be the rest!

                                    Robert Browning

Remember now thy creator in the days of thy youth, while the evil days come not, nor the years draw nigh, when thou shalt say, I have no pleasure in them.

While the sun, or the light, or the moon, or the stars, be not darkened, nor the clouds return after the rain:

In the day when the keepers of the house shall tremble, and the strong men shall bow themselves, and the grinders cease because they are few, and those that look out of the windows be darkened,

And the doors shall be shut in the streets, when the sound of the grinding is low, and he shall rise up at the voice of the bird, and all the daughters of music shall be brought low;

Also when they shall be afraid of that which is high, and fears shall be in the way, and the almond tree shall flourish, and the grasshopper shall be a burden, and desire

shall fail; because man goeth to his long home, and the
mourners go about the streets:

Or ever the silver cord be loosed, or the golden bowl
be broken, or the pitcher be broken at the fountain, or
the wheel broken at the cistern.

Then shall the dust return to the earth as it was: and
the spirit shall return unto God who gave it.

Vanity of vanities, saith the preacher; all is vanity.

Ecclesiastes, Chapter 12

I

The awful shadow of some unseen Power
    Floats though unseen among us, – visiting
    This various world with as inconstant wing
As summer winds that creep from flower to flower, –
Like moonbeams that behind some piny mountain
            shower,
        It visits with inconstant glance
        Each human heart and countenance;
Like hues and harmonies of evening, –
        Like clouds in starlight widely spread, –
        Like memory of music fled, –
        Like aught that for its grace may be
Dear, and yet dearer for its mystery.

II

Spirit of Beauty, that dost consecrate
    With thine own hues all thou dost shine upon
    Of human thought or form, – where art thou gone?
Why dost thou pass away and leave our state,

This dim vast vale of tears, vacant and desolate?
    Ask why the sunlight not for ever
    Weaves rainbows o'er yon mountain-river,
Why aught should fail and fade that once is shown,
    Why fear and dream and death and birth
    Cast on the daylight of this earth
    Such gloom, – why man has such a scope
For love and hate, despondency and hope?

        P. B. Shelley: from the *Hymn to Intellectual Beauty*

When I have fears that I may cease to be
    Before my pen has glean'd my teeming brain,
Before high-piled books, in charact'ry,
    Hold like full garners the full-ripen'd grain;
When I behold, upon the night's starr'd face,
    Huge cloudy symbols of a high romance,
And feel that I may never live to trace
    Their shadows, with the magic hand of chance;
And when I feel, fair creature of an hour!
    That I shall never look upon thee more,
Never have relish in the faery power
    Of unreflecting love! – then on the shore
Of the wide world I stand alone, and think,
Till Love and Fame to nothingness do sink.

        John Keats

When I have fears, as Keats had fears,
Of the moment I'll cease to be,
I console myself with vanished years,
Remembered laughter, remembered tears,
The peace of the changing sea:
And absent friends who are dead and gone –
How happy they are I cannot know,
But happy am I who loved them so.

Noël Coward

Death is not an event of life. Death is not lived through. If by eternity is understood not endless temporal duration but timelessness, then he lives eternally who lives in the present. Our life is endless in the way that our visual field is without limit. The temporal immortality of the human soul, that is, its eternal survival after death, is not only in no way guaranteed, but this assumption will not do for us what we have always tried to make it do. Is the riddle solved by the fact that I survive forever? Is this eternal life not as enigmatic as our present one?

Ludwig Wittgenstein (tr. C. K. Ogden)

My answer to Saint Paul's question 'O death, where is thy sting?' is Saint Paul's own answer: 'The sting of death is sin.' The sin that I mean is the sin of selfishly failing to wish to survive the death of someone with whose life my own life is bound up. This is selfish because the sting of death is less sharp for the person who dies than it is for the bereaved survivor. This is, as I see it, the capital fact about the relation between living and dying. There are two parties to the suffering that death inflicts; and, in the apportionment of this suffering, the survivor takes the brunt.

Arnold Toynbee

Our Friends Go With Us

Our friends go with us as we go
  Down the long path where Beauty wends,
Where all we love forgathers, so
  Why should we fear to join our friends?

Who would survive them to outlast
  His children; to outwear his fame –
Left when the Triumph has gone past –
  To win from Age, not Time, a name?

Then do not shudder at the knife
  That Death's indifferent hand drives home,
But with the Strivers leave the Strife
  Nor, after Cæsar, skulk in Rome.

Oliver St. John Gogarty

Death comes equally to us all, and makes us all equal when it comes. The ashes of an Oak in the Chimney, are no epitaph of that Oak, to tell me how high or how large that was; it tells me not what flocks it sheltered when it stood, nor what men it hurt when it fell. The dust of great persons' graves is speechless too, it says nothing, it distinguishes nothing: As soon the dust of a wretch whom thou wouldest not, as of a Prince whom thou couldest not look upon, will trouble thine eyes, if the wind blow it thither; and when a whirlwind hath blown the dust of the Churchyard into the Church, and the man sweeps out the dust of the Church into the Churchyard, who will undertake to sift those dusts again, and to pronounce, This is the Patrician, this is the noble flower, and this the yeomanly, this the Plebeian bran.

John Donne

It is a thing that every one suffers, even persons of the lowest resolution, of the meanest virtue, of no breeding, of no discourse. Take away but the pomps of death, the disguises and solemn bugbears, the tinsel, and the actings by candle-light, and proper and fantastic ceremonies, the minstrels and the noise-makers, the women and the weepers, the swoonings and the shriekings, the nurses and the physicians, the dark room and the ministers, the kindred and the watchers; and then to die is easy, ready and quitted from its troublesome circumstances. It is the same harmless thing that a poor shepherd suffered yesterday, or a maidservant today; and at the same time in which you die, in that very night a thousand creatures die with you, some wise men, and many fools; and the wisdom of the first will not quit him, and the folly of the latter does not make him unable to die.

Of all the evils of the world which are reproached with an evil character, death is the most innocent of its accusation. For when it is present, it hurts nobody; and when it is absent, it is indeed troublesome, but the trouble is owing to our fears, not the affrighting and mistaken object: and besides this, if it were an evil, it is so transient, that it passes like the instant or undiscerned portion of the present time; and either it is past, or it is not yet; for just when it is, no man hath reason to complain of so insensible, so sudden, so undiscerned a change.

Jeremy Taylor: *Holy Dying*

Adieu! farewell earth's bliss!
This world uncertain is:
Fond are life's lustful joys,
Death proves them all but toys.
None from his darts can fly:
I am sick, I must die.
                    Lord, have mercy on us!

Rich men, trust not in wealth!
Gold cannot buy you health;
Physic himself must fade;
All things to end are made;

The plague full swift goes by:
I am sick, I must die.
        Lord, have mercy on us!

Beauty is but a flower
Which wrinkles will devour;
Brightness falls from the air;
Queens have died young and fair;
Dust hath closed Helen's eye:
I am sick, I must die.
        Lord, have mercy on us!

Strength stoops unto the grave:
Worms feed on Hector brave;
Swords may not fight with fate;
Earth still holds ope her gate;
Come! come! the bells do cry.
I am sick, I must die.
        Lord have mercy on us!

Wit with his wantonness
Tasteth death's bitterness;
Hell's executioner
Hath no ears for to hear
What vain art can reply:
I am sick, I must die.
        Lord, have mercy on us!

Haste, therefore, each degree
To welcome destiny:
Heaven is our heritage,
Earth but a player's stage:
Mount we unto the sky.
I am sick, I must die.
        Lord, have mercy on us!

Thomas Nashe: *Summer's Last Will and Testament*

What If Some Little Paine the Passage Have

... What if some little paine the passage have,
That makes fraile flesh to feare the bitter wave?
Is not short paine well borne, that brings long ease,
And layes the soule to sleepe in quiet grave?
    Sleep after toyle, port after stormie seas,
Ease after warre, death after live does greatly please. ...

                                            Edmund Spenser

"Tis Now Full Tide 'Tween Night and Day'

Leave me, O Love, which reachest but to dust;
And thou, my mind, aspire to higher things;
Grow rich in that which never taketh rust;
Whatever fades, but fading pleasure brings.

Draw in thy beams, and humble all thy might
To that sweet yoke where lasting freedoms be;
Which breaks the clouds and opens forth the light,
That doth both shine and give us sight to see.

O, take fast hold! let that light be thy guide
In this small course which birth draws out to death –
And think how evil becometh him to slide,
Who seeketh heaven, and comes of heavenly breath.

        Then farewell, world; thy uttermost I see:
        Eternal Love, maintain thy life in me.

                                            Sir Philip Sidney

Of Dying Young

But that, perhaps, which anguisheth thee most, is to have
this glorious Pageant of the World removed from thee,
in the Spring and most delicious Season of thy Life; for
though to die be usual, to die young may appear
extraordinary. If the present Fruition of these Things be
unprofitable and vain, What can a long Continuance of
them be? If God had made Life happier, he had also
made it longer. Stranger and new Halcyon, why would
thou longer nestle amidst these unconstant and stormy
Waters? Hast thou not already suffered enough of this
World, but thou must yet endure more? To live long, is
it not to be long troubled? But number thy Years, which
are now . . . and thou shalt find, that whereas Ten have
outlived thee, Thousands have not attained this Age.
One Year is sufficient to behold all the Magnificence of
Nature, nay, even One Day and Night; for more is but
the same brought again. This Sun, that Moon, these Stars,
the varying Dance of the Spring, Summer, Autumn,
Winter, is that very same which the Golden Age did see.
They which have the longest Time lent them to live in,
have almost no Part of it at all, measuring it either by
the Space of Time which is past, when they were not, or
by that which is to come. Why shouldst thou then care,
whether thy Days be many or few, which, when
prolonged to the uttermost, prove, paralleled with
Eternity, as a Tear is to the Ocean? To die young, is to
do that soon, and in some fewer Days, which once thou
must do; it is but the giving over of a Game, that after
never so many Hazards, must be lost.

William Drummond of Hawthornden:
from *The Cypresse Grove*

Perchance hee for whom this *Bell* tolls, may be so ill, as
that he knowes not it tolls for him; And perchance I
may thinke my selfe so much better than I am, as that
they who are about mee, and see my state, may have
caused it to toll for mee, and I know not that. The *Church*
is *Catholike, universall*, so are all her *Actions; All* that she
does, belongs to *all*. When she *baptizes a child*, that action
concernes mee; for that child is thereby connected to
that *Head* which is my *Head* too, and engraffed into that
body, whereof I am a *member*. And when she *buries* a
Man, that action concernes mee: All *mankinde* is of one
Author, and is one *volume;* when one Man dies, one
Chapter is not *torne* out of the *booke*, but *translated* into a
better *language;* and every *Chapter* must be so *translated;*
God emploies several *translators;* some peeces are
translated by *age*, some by *sicknesse*, some by *warre*, some
by *justice;* but *Gods* hand is in every *translation;* and his
hand shall binde up all our scattered leaves againe, for
that *Librarie* where every *booke* shall lie open to one
another: As therefore the *Bell* that rings to a *Sermon*, calls
not upon the *Preacher* onely, but upon the *Congregation*
to come; so this *Bell* calls us all: but how much more
mee, who am brought so neere the *doore* by this *sicknesse*.
There was a *contention* as farre as a *suite*, (in which both
pietie and *dignitie, religion*, and *estimation*, were mingled)
which of the religious *Orders* should ring to *praiers* first
in the *Morning;* and it was *determined*, that *they should
ring first that rose earliest*. If we understand aright the
dignitie of this *Bell* that tolls for our *evening prayer*, wee
would bee glad to make it ours, by rising early, in that
application, that it might bee ours, as wel as his whose
indeed it is. The *Bell* doth toll for him that *thinkes* it
doth; and though it *intermit* againe, yet from that *minute*,
that that occasion wrought upon him, hee is united to
God. Who casts not up his *Eye* to the *Sunne* when it

rises? but who takes off his *Eye* from a *Comet* when that breakes out? Who bends not his *eare* to any *bell*, which upon any occasion rings? but who can remove it from that *bell*, which is passing a *peece of himselfe* out of this *world*? No man is an *Iland*, intire of it selfe; every man is a peece of the *Continent*, a part of the *maine*; if a *Clod* bee washed away by the *Sea, Europe* is the lesse, as well as if a *Promontorie* were, as well as if a *Mannor* of thy *friends* or of *thine owne* were; any mans *death* diminishes *me*, because I am involved in *Mankinde;* And therefore never send to know for whom the *bell* tolls; It tolls for *thee*.

John Donne

Man, proud man,
Drest in a little brief authority,
Most ignorant of what he's most assur'd,
His glassy essence, like an angry ape,
Plays such fantastic tricks before high heaven,
As make the angels weep.

William Shakespeare: *Measure for Measure*

(*Claudio*) The miserable have no other medicine
But only hope:
I have hope to live, and am prepar'd to die.
(*Duke*) Be absolute for death; either death or life
Shall thereby be the sweeter. Reason thus with life:
If I do lose thee, I do lose a thing
That none but fools would keep: a breath thou art
Servile to all the skyey influences,
That dost this habitation, where thou keep'st,
Hourly afflict. Merely, thou art death's fool;
For him thou labour'st by thy flight to shun,
And yet run'st toward him still.

William Shakespeare: *Measure for Measure*

O death, how bitter is the remembrance of thee to a man that is at peace in his possessions, unto the man that hath nothing to distract him, and hath prosperity in all things, and that still hath strength to receive meat! O death, acceptable is thy sentence unto a man that is needy, and that faileth in strength, that is in extreme old age, and is distracted about all things, and is perverse, and hath lost patience! Fear not the sentence of death; remember them that have been before thee, and that come after: this is the sentence from the Lord over all flesh. And why dost thou refuse, when it is the good pleasure of the Most High? Whether it be ten, or a hundred, or a thousand years, there is no inquisition of life in the grave.

Ecclesiasticus, 41

As we grow old, our sense of the value of time becomes vivid. Nothing else, indeed, seems of any consequence. We can never cease wondering that that which has ever been should cease to be. We find many things remain the same: why then should there be change in us. This adds a convulsive grasp of whatever is, a sense of fallacious hollowness in all we see. Instead of the full, pulpy feeling of youth tasting existence and every object in it, all is flat and vapid – a whited sepulchre, fair without but full of ravening and all uncleanness within. The world is a witch that puts us off with false shows and appearances. The simplicity of youth, the confiding expectation, the boundless raptures, are gone: we only think of getting out of it as well as we can, and without any great mischance or annoyance. The flush of illusion, even the complacent retrospect of past joys and hopes, is over: if we can slip out of life without indignity, can escape with little bodily infirmity, and frame our minds to the calm and respectable composure of *still-life* before we return to absolute nothingness, it is as much as we can expect. We do not die wholly at our deaths: we have mouldered away gradually long before. Faculty after faculty, interest after interest, attachment after attachment disappear: we are torn from ourselves while living, year after year sees us no longer the same, and death only consigns the last fragment of what we were to the grave. That we should wear out by slow stages, and dwindle at last into nothing, is not wonderful, when even in our prime our strongest impressions leave little trace for the moment, and we are the creatures of petty circumstance.

William Hazlitt

4

Death, the Dead and the Dying

After the Death of a Friend

You died, and made but little of it! –
Why then should I, when called to doff it,
Drop, and renounce this worm-holed raiment,
Shrink edgewise off from its grey claimant?
Rather say, when I am Time – outrun,
As you did: Take me, and have done,
Inexorable, instatiate one!

Thomas Hardy

Some hang above the tombs,
Some weep in empty rooms,
I, when the iris blooms,
          Remember.

*   *   *

I, when the cyclamen
Opens her buds again,
Rejoice a moment – then
          Remember.

Mary Coleridge

Death, be not proud, though some have callèd thee
    Mighty and dreadful, for thou art not so;
    For those whom thou think'st thou dost overthrow
Die not, poor Death, nor yet canst thou kill me.
From rest and sleep, which but thy pictures be,
    Much pleasure – then, from thee much more must
flow;
    And soonest our best men with thee do go,
Rest of their bones and soul's delivery.
Thou'rt slave to fate, chance, kings and desperate men,
    And dost with poison, war, and sickness dwell;
    And poppy or charms can make us sleep as well,
And better than thy stroke. Why swell'st thou then?
      One short sleep past, we wake eternally,
      And death shall be no more. Death, thou shalt die.

John Donne

Margaritae Sorori, I.M.

A late lark twitters from the quiet skies;
And from the west,
Where the sun, his day's work ended,
Lingers as in content
There falls on the old, gray city
An influence luminous and serene,
A shining peace.

The smoke ascends
In a rosy-and-golden haze. The spires
Shine, and are changed. In the valley
Shadows rise. The lark sings on. The sun,
Closing his benediction,

Sinks, and the darkening air
Thrills with a sense of the triumphing night –
Night with her train of stars
And her great gift of sleep.

So be my passing!
My task accomplished and the long day done,
My wages taken, and in my heart
Some late lark singing,
Let me be gathered to the quiet west,
The sundown splendid and serene,
Death.

W. E. Henley

We are too apt to consider death as the greatest evil,
instead of the greatest good. It is the termination of all
pains and the beginning of all pleasures. It is a release
from a thousand vexations and uncertainties, from which
even the most prosperous are not free, to a state in which
there is no solicitude and woe; and where the righteous
are placed far beyond the reach of malice or misfortune.
If death be so great a good, it can be nothing but a false

view of the subject, or the dire forebodings of a guilty
conscience, that can make the event itself an object of
terror and dismay.

Robert Fellowes: from *A Brief Treatise on Death*

I am the Reaper.
All things with heedful hook
Silent I gather.
Pale roses touched with the spring,
Tall corn in summer,
Fruits rich with autumn, and frail winter blossoms –
Reaping, still reaping –
All things with heedful hook
Timely I gather.

I am the Sower.
All the unbodied life
Runs through my seed-sheet.
Atom with atom wed,
Each quickening the other,
Fall through my hands, ever changing, still changeless.
Ceaselessly sowing,
Life, incorruptible life,
Flows from my seed-sheet.

Maker and breaker,
I am the ebb and the flood,
Here and Hereafter.
Sped through the tangle and coil
Of infinite nature,

Viewless and soundless I fashion all being.
Taker and giver,
I am the womb and the grave,
The Now and the Ever.

W E Henley

2 Death the Consequence of the Fall

O wretched offspring! O unhappy state
Of all mankind, by me betrayed to fate!
Born, through my crime, to be offenders first,
And, for those sins they could not shun, accurst.
Why is life forced on man; who, might he choose,
Would not accept what he, with pain, must lose?
Unknowing, he receives it, and, when known
He thinks it his, and values it, 'tis gone.
Behold of every age: ripe manhood see,
Decrepit years, and helpless infancy:
Those who, by lingering sickness, lose their breath;
And those who, by despair, suborn their death.
See yon mad fools who, for some trivial right,
For love, or for mistaken honour, fight.
See those, more mad, who throw their lives away
In needless wars: the stakes which monarchs lay
When for each other's provinces they play.
Then as if earth too narrow were for fate,
On open seas their quarrels they debate;
In hollow wood they floating armies bear,
And force imprisoned winds to bing 'em near.
Who would the miseries of man foreknow?

Not knowing, we but share out part of woe.
Now, we the fate of future ages bear;
And ere the birth, behold our dead appear.
The deaths thou showest are forced and full of strife,
Cast headlong from the precipice of life.
Is there no smooth descent? no painless way
Of kindly mixing with out native clay?
There is, but rarely shall that path be trod
Which, without horror, leads to death's abode.
Some few, by temperance taught, approaching slow,
To distant fate by easy journeys go.
Gently they lay'em down, as evening sheep
On their own woolly fleeces softly sleep.
So noiseless would I live, such death to find,
Like timely fruit, not shaken by the wind
But ripely dropping from the sapless bough,
And, dying, nothing to myself would owe.
Thus, daily changing, with a duller taste
Of lessening joys I, by degrees, would waste,
Still quitting ground by unperceived decay,
And steal myself from life, and melt away.

John Dryden

... When thou has lived to that Age thou desirest, or one of *Plato's* Years, so soon as the last of thy Days riseth above thy Horizon, thou wilt then, as now, demand longer Respite, and expect more to come. The oldest are most unwilling to die. It is Hope of long Life that maketh Life seem short. Heaven foreknowing imminent Harms, taketh those which it loves to itself before they fall forth.

Death in Youth is like the leaving a superfluous Feast before the drunken Cups be presented. Life is a journey in a dusty Way, the furthest Rest is Death, in this some go more heavily burdened than others: Swift and active Pilgrims come to the End of it in the Morning or at Noon, which Tortoise-paced Wretches, clogged with the fragmentary Rubbish of this World, scarce with great Travel crawl unto at Midnight. Days are not to be esteemed after the Number of them, but after the Goodness. More Compass maketh not a Sphere more compleat, but as round is a little as a large Ring; nor is that Musician most praiseworthy who hath longest played, but he in measured Accents who hath made sweetest Melody.

William Drummond

That time of life thou mayst in me behold,
When yellow leaves, or none, or few do hang
Upon those boughs which shake against the cold,
Bare ruined choirs, where late the sweet birds sang.
In me thou seest the twilight of such day,
As after sunset fadeth in the west,
Which by and by black night doth take away,
Death's second self that seals up all in rest.
In me thou seest the glowing of such fire,
That on the ashes of his youth doth lie,

As the death-bed, whereon it must expire,
Consumed with that which it was nourished by.
   This thou perceiv'st, which makes thy love more
       strong,
   To love that well, which thou must leave ere long.

                              William Shakespeare

The Death-Bed

We watched her breathing through the night,
Her breathing soft and low,
As in her breast the wave of life
Kept heaving to and fro!

So silently we seemed to speak –
So slowly moved about!
As we had lent her half our powers
To eke her living out!

Our very hopes belied our fears
Our fears our hoped belied –
We thought her dying when she slept,
And sleeping when she died!

For when the morn came dim and sad –
And chill with early showers,
Her quiet eyelids closed – she had
Another morn than ours!

                                 Thomas Hood

On the Death of Emily Jane Brontë

My darling, thou wilt never know
The grinding agony of woe
   That we have borne for thee.
Thus may we consolation tear
E'en from the depth of our despair
   And wasting misery.

The nightly anguish thou art spared
When all the crushing truth is bared
   To the awakening mind,
When the galled heart is pierced with grief,
Till wildly it implores relief,
   But small relief can find.

Nor know'st thou what it is to lie
Looking forth with streaming eye
     On life's lone wilderness.
   'Weary, weary, dark and drear,
How shall I the journey bear,
   The burden and distress?'

Then since thou art spared such pain
We will not wish thee here again;
   He that lives must mourn.
God help us through our misery
And gives us rest and joy with thee
   When we reach our bourne!

Charlotte Brontë

God took her to himself. She suffered very little pain, and was spared the misery of knowing she was about to leave us; she was smilingly assuring me she was better to within a few minutes of the last. . . .

Then came what my heart will keep till I see her again, and longer, the most perfect expression of her love to me within my whole knowledge of her. Always smilingly, happily, and with a face like a girl's, and in a few minutes she died in my arms, her head on my cheek. God took her to himself as you would lift a sleeping child from a dark, weary bed into the light.

Robert Browning to a friend

Sleep, O cluster of friends,
Sleep! – or only when May,
Brought by the west-wind returns
Back to your native heaths,
And the plover is heard on the moors,
Yearly awake to behold
The opening summer, the sky,
The shining moorland – to hear
The drowsy bee, as of old,
Hum o'er the thyme, the grouse
Call from the heather in bloom!
Sleep, or only for this
Break your united repose!

So I sang; but the Muse
Shaking her head, took the harp
– Stern interrupted my strain,
Angrily smote on the chords. . . .

... April showers
Rush o'er the Yorkshire moors.
Stormy, through driving mist,
Loom the blurr'd hills; the rain
Lashes the newly made grave.

Unquiet souls!
– In the dark fermentation of earth,
In the never idle workshop of nature,
In the eternal movement,
Ye shall find yourselves again.

Matthew Arnold: from *Haworth Churchyard*

Death

Death, that struck when I was most confiding
In my certain Faith of Joy to be,
Strike again, Time's withered branch dividing
From the fresh root of Eternity!

Leaves, upon Time's branch, were growing brightly,
Full of sap and full of silver dew,
Birds, beneath its shelter, gathered nightly;
Daily, round its flowers, the wild bees flew.

Sorrow passed and plucked the golden blossom,
Guilt stripped off the foliage in its pride;
But, within its parent's kindly bosom,
Flowed forever Life's restoring tide.

Little mourned I for the parted Gladness,
For the vacant nest and silent song;
Hope was there and laughed me out of sadness,
Whispering, 'Winter will not linger long.'

Emily Brontë

Yes, holy be thy resting place
Wherever thou may'st lie;
The sweetest winds breathe on thy face,
The softest of the sky.

And will not guardian Angels send
Kind dreams and thoughts of love,
Though I no more may watchful bend
Thy longed repose above?

And will not heaven itself bestow
A beam of glory there
That summer's grass more green may grow,
And summer's flowers more fair?

Farewell, farewell, 'tis hard to part
Yet, loved one, it must be:
I would not rend another heart
Not even by blessing thee.

Go! We must break affection's chain,
Forget the hopes of years:
Nay, grieve not – willest thou remain
To waken wilder tears?

This wild breeze with thee and me,
Roved in the dawning day:
And thou shouldest be where it shall be
Ere evening, far away.

Emily Brontë

A Wish

... I ask not each kind soul to keep
Tearless, when of my death he hears.
Let those who will, if any, weep!
There are worse plagues on earth than tears....

... Spare me the whispering, crowded room,
The friends who come, and gape, and go;
The ceremonious air of gloom –
All, which makes death a hideous show!

Nor bring, to see me cease to live,
Some doctor full of phrase and fame,
To shake his sapient head, and give
The ill he cannot cure a name.

Nor fetch, to take the accustom'd toll
Of the poor sinner bound for death,
His brother-doctor of the soul,
To canvass with official breath

The future and its viewless things –
That undiscover'd mystery
Which one who feels death's winnowing wings
Must needs read clearer, sure, than he!

Being none of these; but let me be,
While all around in silence lies,
Moved to the window near, and see
Once more, before my dying eyes,

Bathed in the sacred dews of morn
The wide aerial landscape spread –
The world which was ere I was born,
The world which lasts when I am dead;

Which never was the friend of *one*,
Nor promised love it could not give,
But lit for all its generous sun,
And lived itself, and made us live.

There let me gaze, till I become
In soul, with what I gaze on, wed!
To feel the universe my home;
To have before my mind – instead

Of the sick room, the mortal strife,
The turmoil for a little breath –
The pure eternal course of life,
Not human combatings with death!

Thus feeling, gazing, might I grow
Composed, refresh'd, ennobled, clear;
Then willing let my spirit go
To work or wait elsewhere or here!

Matthew Arnold

Be near me when the sensuous frame
   Is rack'd with pangs that conquer trust;
   And Time, a maniac scattering dust,
And Life, a Fury slinging flame.

Be near me when my faith is dry,
   And men the flies of latter spring,
   That lay their eggs, and sting and sing,
And weave their petty cells and die.

Be near me when I fade away,
   To point the term of human strife,
   And on the low dark verge of life
The twilight of eternal day.

Be near me when my light is low,
   When the blood creeps, and the nerves prick
   And tingle; and the heart is sick,
And all the wheels of Being slow.

                    Alfred, Lord Tennyson

The Bourne

Underneath the growing grass,
   Underneath the living flowers,
   Deeper than the sound of showers:
   There we shall not count the hours
By the shadows as they pass.

Youth and health will be but vain,
  Beauty reckoned of no worth:
  There a very little girth
  Can hold round what once the earth
Seemed too narrow to contain.

                                                              Christina Rossetti

Grass of levity,
Span in brevity,
Flowers' felicity,
Fire of misery,
Winds' stability,
Is mortality.

                                                              Anon.

Cut Grass

Cut grass lies frail:
Brief is the breath
Mown stalks exhale.
Long, long the death

It dies in the white hours
Of young-leafed June
With chestnut flowers,
With hedges snowlike strewn,

White lilac bowed,
Lost lanes of Queen Anne's lace,
And that high-builded cloud
Moving at summer's pace.

Philip Larkin

. . . It is therefore Death alone that can suddenly make
man to know himselfe. He tells the proud and insolent,
that they are but Abjects, and humbles them at the
instant; makes them crie, complaine, and repent, yea,
even to hate their forepassed happinesse. He takes the
account of the rich, and proves him a beggar; a naked
beggar, which hath interest in nothing, but in the gravell
that fills his mouth. He holds a glasse before the eyes of
the most beautiful, and makes them see therein their
deformitie and rottennesse, and they acknowledge it.

O eloquent, just, and mighty Death! whom none
could advise, thou has perswaded; what none hath dared
thou hast done; and whom all the world hath flattered,
thou only has cast out of the world and despised: thou
hast drawne together all the farre-stretched greatnesse,
all the pride, crueltie, and ambition of man, and covered
it all over with these two narrow words, *Hic jacet.* (Here
Lies).

Sir Walter Raleigh

Plaint

Dark, deep, and cold the current flows
Unto the sea where no wind blows,
Seeking the land which no one knows. . . .

Though myriads go with him who goes,
Alone he goes where no wind blows,
Unto the land which no one knows.

For all must go where no wind blows,
And none can go for him who goes,
None, none return whence no one knows. . . .

O shoreless Deep, where no wind blows!
And, thou, O Land which no one knows! –
That God is All, His shadow shows!

Ebenezer Elliot

On Mrs. Clarke
Jane Clarke – died April 27, 1757, aged 31

Lo! where this silent marble weeps,
A Friend, a wife, a mother sleeps:
A heart, within whose sacred cell
The peaceful virtues loved to dwell.
Affection warm, and faith sincere,
And soft humanity were there.
In agony, in death, resigned,
She felt the wound she left behind,
Her infant image here below,
Sits smiling on a father's woe:

Whom what awaits, while yet he strays
Along the lonely vale of days?
A pang, to secret sorrow dear;
A sigh; an unavailing tear;
Till time shall every grief remove,
With life, with memory, and with love.

Thomas Gray

Mater Dolorosa

I'd a dream to-night
    As I fell asleep,
O! the touching sight
    Makes me still to weep:
Of my little lad,
Gone to leave me sad,
Ay, the child I had,
    But was not to keep.

As in heaven high,
    I my child did seek,
There in train came by
    Children fair and meek,
Each in lily white,
With a lamp alight;
Each was clear to sight,
    But they did not speak.

Then, a little sad,
    Came my child in turn,
But the lamp he had
    O it did not burn!

He, to clear my doubt,
Said, half-turned about,
'Your tears put it out;
    Mother, never mourn.'

William Barnes

On Solomon Pavy
A Child of Queen Elizabeth's Chapel

Weep with me, all you that read
    This little story;
And know, for whom a tear you shed
    Death's self is sorry.
'Twas a child that so did thrive
    In grace and feature,
As Heaven and Nature seemed to strive
    Which owned the creature.
Years he numbered scarce thirteen
    When Fates turned cruel,
Yet three filled Zodiacs had he been
    The Stage's jewel;
And did act (what now we moan)
    Old men so duly,
As sooth the Parcae thought him one,
    He played so truly.
So, by error, to his fate
    They all consented;
But, viewing him since, alas, too late!
    They have repented;

And have sought, to give new birth,
    In baths to steep him;
But, being so much too good for earth,
    Heaven vows to keep him.

                         Ben Jonson

On a Child

Here, freed from pain, secure from misery, lies
A child, the darling of his parents' eyes:
A gentler Lamb ne'er sported on the plain,
A fairer flower will never bloom again:
Few were the days allotted to his breath;
Now let him sleep in peace his night of death.

                         Thomas Gray

On My First Son

Farewell, thou child of my right hand, and joy;
My sin was too much hope of thee, loved boy:
Seven years thou wert lent to me, and I thee pay,
Exacted by thy fate, on the first day.
O, could I lose all father, now! For why
Will man lament the state he should envy?
To have so soon 'scaped world's, and flesh's rage,
And, if no other misery, yet age!

Rest in soft peace, and, ask'd, say here doth lie
Ben Jonson his best piece of poetry:
For whose sake, henceforth, all his vows be such,
As what he loves may never like too much.

                                                           Ben Jonson

[*To My Dearest Brother*]

. . . In perfect honour, perfect truth,
And gentleness to all mankind,
You trod the golden paths of youth,
Then left the world and youth behind.
Ah no! – 'Tis we who fade and fail –
And you, from Time's slow torments free,
Shall pass from strength to strength, and scale
The steeps of immortality.

Dear heart, in that serener air,
If blessed soul may backward gaze,
Some slender nook of memory spare
For our old happy moorland days.
I sit alone, and musing fills
My breast with pain that shall not die,
Till once again, o'er greener hills
We ride together, you and I.

            John Buchan: from *Fratri Dilectissimo W.H.B.*

In Memory of My Dear Grandchild Elizabeth Bradstreet,
  who deceased August 1665, being a year and a half old.

Farewell dear babe, my heart's too much content,
Farewell sweet babe the pleasure of mine eye,
Farewell fair flower that for a space was lent,
Then ta'en away unto Eternity.
Blest babe, why should I once bewail thy fate
Or sigh thy days so soon were terminate,
Sith thou art settled in an Everlasting state?
By nature trees do rot when they are grown,
And plums and apples thoroughly ripe do fall,
And corn and grass are in their season mown,
And time brings down what is both strong and tall.
But plants new set to be eradicate,
And buds new blown to have so short a date,
Is by His hand alone that guides nature and fate.

                                        Anne Bradstreet

Like Buds appearing ere the Frosts are past,
To become Man he made such fatal hast,
And to Perfection labour'd so to climb,
Preventing slow Experience and Time,
That 'tis no wonder Death our Hopes beguil'd;
He's seldom Old, that will not be a Child.

                                        Edmund Waller

To a Little Child in Death

Dear, if little feet make little journeys,
   Thine should not be far;
      Though beyond the faintest star,
      Past earth's last bar,
      Where angels are,
        Thou hast to travel –
Cross the far blue spaces of the sea,
Climb above the tallest tree,
Higher up than many mountains be;
   Sure there is some shorter way for thee,
Since little feet make little journeys.

Then, if smallest limbs are soonest weary,
   Thou should'st soon be there;
      Stumbling up the golden stair,
      Where the angels' shining hair
        Brushes dust from baby faces.
      Very, very gently cling
      To a silver-edged wing,
        And peep from under.
      Then thou'lt see the King,
      Then will many voices sing,
        And thou wilt wonder.
      Wait a little while
      For Him to smile,
        Who calleth thee.
      He who calleth all,
      Both great and small,
      From over mountain, star and sea,
   Doth call the smallest soonest to His knee,
Since smallest limbs are soonest weary.

                       Charlotte Mew

To a Child in Death

You would have scoffed if we had told you yesterday
    Love made us feel, or so it was with me, like some
        great bird
      Trying to hold and shelter you in its strong
        wing; –
A gay little shadowy smile would have tossed us back
        such a solemn word,
      And it was not for that you were listening
      When so quietly you slipped away
With half the music of the world unheard.
What shall we do with this strange summer, meant for
        you, –
      Dear, if we see the winter through,
      What shall be done with spring?
This, this is the victory of the Grave; here is death's
        sting,
That it is not strong enough, our strongest wing.

But what of His, who like a Father pitieth?
His Son was also, once, a little thing,
The wistfullest child that every drew breath,
Chased by a sword from Bethlehem and in the busy
        house at Nazareth
Playing with little rows of nails, watching the
        carpenter's hammer swing,
Long years before His hands and feet were tied
And by a hammer and the three great nails He died,
      Of Youth, of Spring,
Of sorrow, of loneliness, of victory the King,
      Under the shadow of that wing.

Charlotte Mew

The sun is soon to rise as bright
As if the night had brought no sorrow.
That grief belonged to me alone,
The sun shines on a common morrow.

You must not shut the night inside you,
But endlessly in light the dark immerse.
A tiny lamp has gone out in my tent –
I bless the flame that warms the universe.

> Friedrich Rückert, *Songs on the Death of Children*
> (translated D. J. Enright)

All his beauty, wit and grace
Lie forever in one place.
He who sang and sprang and moved
Now, in death, is only loved.

> Alice Thomas Ellis, 'To Joshua',
> dedication prefixed to *The Birds of the Air*.

– No, no, no life!
Why should a dog, a horse, a rat have life,
And thou no breath at all? Thou'lt come no more,
Never, never, never, never, never!

> William Shakespeare: *King Lear*

Autumn

There is a wind where the rose was;
Cold rain where sweet grass was;
    And clouds like sheep
    Stream o'er the steep
Grey skies were the lark was.

Nought gold where you hair was;
Nought warm where your hand was;
    But phantom, forlorn,
    Beneath the thorn,
Your ghost where your face was,
Sad winds where your voice was;
Tears, tears where my heart was;
    And ever with me,
    Child, ever with me,
Silence where hope was.

                              Walter De La Mare

On a Dead Child

Perfect little body, without fault or stain on thee,
    With promise of strength and manhood full and fair!
        Though cold and stark and bare,
The bloom and the charm of life doth awhile remain on
        thee.

Thy mother's treasure wert thou; – alas! no longer
    To visit her heart with wondrous joy; to be
        Thy father's pride; – ah, he
Must gather his faith together, and his strength make
        stronger.

To me, as I move thee now in the last duty,
    Dost thou with a turn or gesture anon respond;
        Startling my fancy fond
With a chance attitude of the head, a freak of beauty.

Thy hand clasps, as 'twas wont, my finger, and holds it:
    But the grasp is the clasp of Death, heartbreaking and
        stiff;
        Yet feels to my hand as if
'Twas still thy will, thy pleasure and trust that enfolds it.

So I lay thee there, thy sunken eyelids closing, –
    Go lie thou there in thy coffin, thy last little bed! –
        Propping thy wise, sad head,
Thy firm, pale hands across thy chest disposing.

So quiet! doth the change content thee? – Death,
        whither hath he taken thee?
    To a world, do I think, that rights the disaster of this?
        The vision of which I miss,
Who weep for the body, and wish to warm thee and
        awaken thee?

Ah! little at best can all our hopes avail us
    To lift this sorrow, or cheer us, when in the dark,
        Unwilling, alone we embark,
And the things we have seen and have known and have
        heard of, fail us.

                                                    Robert Bridges

For a Child Born Dead

What ceremony can we fit
You into now? If you had come
Out of a warm and noisy room
To this, there'd be an opposite
For us to know you by. We could
Imagine you in lively mood

And then look at the other side,
The mood drawn out of you, the breath
Defeated by the power of death.
But we have never seen you stride
Ambitiously the world we know.
You could not come and yet you go.

But there is nothing now to mar
Your clear refusal of our world.
Not in our memories can we mould
You or distort your character.
Then all our consolation is
That grief can be as pure as this.

                                        Elizabeth Jennings

. . . Turn from him, turn, officious thought!
Officious thought presents again
The thousand little acts he wrought,
Which wound my heart with soothing pain:
His looks, his winning gestures rise,
His waving hands, and laughing eyes.

Those waving hands no more shall move,
Those laughing eyes shall smile no more:
He cannot now engage our love,
With sweet insinuating power
Our weak unguarded hearts insnare,
And rival his Creator there. . . .

C. Wesley: *On the Death of his Son*

For the Fallen

With proud thanksgiving, a mother for her children,
England mourns for her dead across the sea.
Flesh of her flesh they were, spirit of her spirit,
Fallen in the cause of the free.

Solemn the drums thrill: Death august and royal
Sings sorrow up into immortal spheres.
There is music in the midst of desolation
And glory that shines upon our tears.

They went with songs to the battle, they were young,
Straight of limb, true of eye, steady and aglow,
They were staunch to the end against odds uncounted,
They fell with their faces to the foe.

They shall grow not old, as we that are left grow old:
Age shall not weary them, nor the years condemn.
At the going down of the sun and in the morning
We will remember them.

They mingle not with their laughing comrades again;
They sit no more at familiar tables of home;
They have no lot in our labour of the day-time;
They sleep beyond England's foam.

But where our desires are and our hopes profound,
Felt as a well-spring that is hidden from sight,
To the innermost heart of their own land they are
    known
As the stars are known to the Night;

As the stars that shall be bright when we are dust,
Moving in marches upon the heavenly plain,
As the stars that are starry in the time of our darkness,
To the end, to the end, they remain.

Laurence Binyon: from The Four Years, 1919.

Here Dead Lie We

Here dead lie we because we did not choose
    To live and shame the land from which we sprung.
Life, to be sure, is nothing much to lose;
    But young men think it is, and we were young.

A. E. Housman

The Soldier

If I should die, think only this of me:
  That there's some corner of a foreign field
That is for ever England. There shall be
  In that rich earth a richer dust concealed;
A dust whom England bore, shaped, made aware,
  Gave, once, her flowers to love, her ways to roam,
A body of England's, breathing English air,
  Washed by the rivers, blest by suns of home.

And think, this heart, all evil shed away,
  A pulse in the eternal mind, no less
    Gives somewhere back the thoughts by England
      given;
Her sights and sounds; dreams happy as her day;
  And laughter, learnt of friends; and gentleness,
    In hearts at peace, under an English heaven.

Rupert Brooke

The Dead

These hearts were woven of human joys and cares,
  Washed marvellously with sorrow, swift to mirth.
The years had given them kindness. Dawn was theirs,
  And sunset, and the colours of the earth.
These had seen movement, and heard music; known
  Slumber and waking; loved; gone proudly friended;
Felt the quick stir of wonder; sat alone;
  Touched flowers and furs and cheeks. All this is
    ended.

There are waters blown by changing winds to laughter
And lit by the rich skies, all day. And after,
Frost, with a gesture, stays the waves that dance
    And wandering loveliness. He leaves a white
Unbroken glory, a gathered radiance,
    A width, a shining peace, under the night.

                                        Rupert Brooke

Smile, Death

Smile, Death, see I smile as I come to you
Straight from the road and the moor that I leave
        behind,
Nothing on earth to me was like this wind-blown
        space,
Nothing was like the road, but at the end there was a
        vision or a face
    And the eyes were not always kind.

    Smile, Death, as you fasten the blades to my feet for
        me,
On, on let us skate past the sleeping willows dusted with
        snow;
Fast, fast down the frozen stream, with the moor and
        the road and the vision behind,
    (Show me your face, why the eyes are kind!)
And we will not speak of life or believe in it or
        remember it as we go.

                                        Charlotte Mew

. . . And how beguile you? Death has no repose
    Warmer and deeper than that Orient sand
Which hides the beauty and bright faith of those
    Who made the Golden Journey to Samarkand.

And now they wait and whiten peaceably,
    Those conquerors, those poets, those so fair:
They know time comes, not only you and I,
    But the whole world shall whiten, here or there;

When those long caravans that cross the plain
    With dauntless feet and sound of silver bells
Put forth no more for glory or for gain,
    Take no more solace from the palm-girt wells.

When the great markets by the sea shut fast
    All that calm Sunday that goes on and on:
When even lovers find their peace at last,
    And Earth is but a star, that once had shone.

James Elroy Flecker: The Golden Journey to Samarkand:
                                       Prologue

Do Not Go Gentle into That Good Night

Do not go gentle into that good night,
Old age should burn and rave at close of day;
Rage, rage against the dying of the light.

Though wise men at their end know dark is right,
Because their words had forked no lightning they
Do not go gentle into that good night.

Good men, the last wave by, crying how bright
Their frail deeds might have danced in a green bay,
Rage, rage against the dying of the light.

Wild men who caught and sang the sun in flight,
And learn, too late, they grieved it on its way,
Do not go gentle into that good night.

Grave men, near death, who see with blinding sight
Blind eyes could blaze like meteors and be gay,
Rage, rage against the dying of the light.

And you, my father, there on the sad height,
Curse, bless, me now with your fierce tears, I pray.
Do not go gentle into that good night.
Rage, rage against the dying of the light.

                                        Dylan Thomas

Lights Out

I have come to the borders of sleep,
The unfathomable deep
Forest where all must lose
Their way, however straight,
Or winding, soon or late;
They cannot choose.

Many a road and track
That, since the dawn's first crack,
Up to the forest brink,
Deceived the travellers,
Suddenly now blurs,
And in they sink.

Here love ends,
Despair, ambition ends;
All pleasure and all trouble,
Although most sweet or bitter,
Here ends in sleep that is sweeter
Than tasks most noble.

There is not any book
Or face of dearest look
That I would not turn from now
To go into the unknown
I must enter, and leave, alone,
I know not how.

The tall forest towers;
Its cloudy foliage lowers
Ahead, shelf above shelf;
Its silence I hear and obey
That I may lose my way
And myself.

Edward Thomas

Music, when soft voices die,
Vibrates in the memory;
Odours, when sweet violets sicken,
Live within the sense they quicken.

Rose leaves, when the rose is dead,
Are heaped for the beloved's bed;
And so thy thoughts, when thou art gone,
Love itself shall slumber on.

P. B. Shelley

Fare Well

When I lie where shades of darkness
Shall no more assail mine eyes,
Nor the rain make lamentation
        When the wind sighs;
How will fare the world whose wonder
Was the very proof of me?
Memory fades, must the remembered
        Perishing be?

Oh, when this my dust surrenders
Hand, foot, lip, to dust again,
May these loved and loving faces
        Please other men!
May the rusting harvest hedgerow
Still the Traveller's Joy entwine,
And as happy children gather
        Posies once mine.

Look thy last on all things lovely,
Every hour. Let no night
Seal thy sense in deathly slumber
    Till to delight
Thou have paid thy utmost blessing;
Since that all things thou wouldst praise
Beauty took from those who loved them
    In other days.

Walter De La Mare

Rest

O Earth, lie heavily upon her eyes;
Seal her sweet eyes weary of watching, Earth;
    Lie close around her; leave no room for mirth
With its harsh laughter, nor for sound of sighs.
She hath no questions, she hath no replies,
    Hushed in and curtained with a blessed dearth
    Of all that irked her from the hour of birth;
With stillness that is almost Paradise.
Darkness more clear than noonday holdeth her,
    Silence more musical than any song;
Even her very heart has ceased to stir:
Until the morning of Eternity
Her rest shall not begin nor end, but be;
    And when she wakes she will not think it long.

Christina Rossetti

Nay why not this? A surer thing is Death
By far than sleep: That nightly drowsy Mist
Which climbs into thy Braine to give Thee Rest,
May by the way obstruct thy feeble Breath.

The Day is gone; and well, if only gone,
Is it not lost? Cast up thy scorn and know
Art so much neerer Heaven as Thou art to
Thy Death; or did thy life without Thee run?

Alas it ran, and for me would not stay,
Who waited on my fruitless Vanities.
I might have travel'd far since I did rise,
In praying and in studying hard to-day.

Great Lord of Life and Time, reprieve me still,
Whom My owne Sentence hath condemn'd; That I
May learne to live my Life before I die,
And teach my owne, to follow Thy Sweet Will.

                                        Joseph Beaumont

Death

One night as I lay on my bed,
And sleep on fleeting foot had fled,
Because, no doubt, my mind was heavy
With concern for my last journey:

I got me up and called for water,
That I might wash, and so feel better;
But before I wet my eyes so dim,
There was Death on the bowl's rim.

I went to church that I might pray,
Thinking sure he'd keep away;
But before I got on to my feet,
There sat Death upon my seat.

To my chamber then I hied,
Thinking sure he'd keep outside;
But though I firmly locked the door,
Death came from underneath the floor.

The to sea I rowed a boat,
Thinking surely Death can't float;
But before I reached the deep,
Death was captain of the ship.

Anon From the Welsh (trans. Aneirin Talfan Davies)

Either death is a state of nothingness, or, as men say, there
is a change of the soul from this world to another. Now,
if you suppose that there is no consciousness, but a sleep
like the sleep of him who is undisturbed even by the
sight of dreams, then to die is gain, for eternity is only a
single night. But if death is the journey to another place,
where, as men say, all the dead are, what good can be
greater than this?

If, when the pilgrim arrives in the world below, he is delivered from the professors of justice in this world, and finds the true judges who are said to give judgment there, that pilgrimage will be worth the making. What would not a man give if he could converse with Orpheus and Homer? Nay; if this be true, let me die again and again.

I shall have a wonderful interest in the place where I can converse with the heroes of old. I shall be able to continue my search into knowledge; I shall find out who is wise and who pretends to be wise and is not. What would not a man give, O judges, to be able to examine the leader of the great Trojan expedition, or Odysseus, or numberless others? What infinite delight would there be in asking them questions, for in that world they do not put a man to death for this – certainly not.

Wherefore, O judges, be of good cheer about death, and know this of a truth – that to a good man no evil thing can happen.

Plato: from the *Phaedo*

Death May Be . . .

Death may be very gentle after all:
He turns his face away from arrogant knights
Who fling themselves against him in their fights;
But to the loveliest he loves to call.
And he has with him those whose ways were mild
And beautiful; and many a little child.

Oliver St. John Gogarty

Death

Nor dread nor hope attend
A dying animal;
A man awaits his end
Dreading and hoping all;
Many times he died,
Many times rose again.
A great man in his pride
Confronting murderous men
Casts derision upon
Supersession of breath;
He knows death to the bone –
Man has created death.

W. B. Yeats

I strove with none, for none was worth my strife.
Nature I loved and, next to Nature, Art:
I warmed both hands before the fire of life:
It sinks, and I am ready to depart.

Walter Savage Landor

Death stands above me, whispering low
   I know not what into my ear:
Of his strange language all I know
   Is, there is not a word of fear.

Walter Savage Landor

The Hour of Death

Be careful, then, and be gentle about death.
For it is hard to die, it is difficult to go through
the door, even when it opens.

And the poor dead, when they have left the walled
and silvery city of the now hopeless body
where are they to go, Oh where are they to go?

They linger in the shadow of the earth.
The earth's long conical shadow is full of souls
that cannot find the way across the sea of change.

Be kind, Oh be kind to your dead
and give them a little encouragement
and help them to build their little ship of death.

For the soul has a long, long journey after death
to the sweet home of pure oblivion.
Each needs a little ship, a little ship
and the proper store of meal for the longest journey.

Oh, from out of your heart
provide for your dead once more, equip them
like departing mariners, lovingly.

                    D. H. Lawrence: *All Soul's Day*

The Ship of Death

Have you built your ship of death, oh have you?
Oh build your ship of death, for you will need it.

Now in the twilight, sit by the invisible sea
Of peace, and build your little ship
Of death, that will carry the soul
On its last journey, on and on, so still
So beautiful, over the last of seas.

When the day comes, that will come.
Oh think of it in the twilight peacefully!
The last day, and the setting forth
On the longest journey, over the hidden sea
To the last wonder of oblivion

Oblivion, the last wonder!
When we have trusted ourselves entirely
To the unknown, and are taken up
Out of our little ships of death
Into pure oblivion.

Oh build your ship of death, be building it now
With dim, calm thoughts and quiet hands
Putting its timbers together in the dusk,
Rigging its mast with the silent, invisible sail
That will spread in death to the breeze
Of the kindness of the cosmos, that will waft
The little ship with its soul to the wonder-goal.

Ah, if you want to live in peace on the face of the earth
Then build your ship of death, in readiness
For the longest journey, over the last of seas.

                                    D. H. Lawrence

Song of Death

Sing the song of death, oh sing it!
For without the song of death, the song of life
becomes pointless and silly.

Sing then the song of death, and the longest journey
and what the soul carries with him, and what he leaves
    behind
and how he finds the darkness that enfolds him into
    utter peace
at last, at last, beyond innumerable seas.

                                    D. H. Lawrence

5

Mourning

Twilight

Twilight it is, and the far woods are dim, and the rooks
cry and call.
Down in the valley the lamps, and the mist, and a star
over all,
There by the rick, where they thresh, is the drone at an
end,
Twilight it is, and I travel the road with my friend.

I think of the friends who are dead, who were dear long
ago in the past,
Beautiful friends who are dead, though I know that
death cannot last;
Friends with the beautiful eyes that the dust has defiled,
Beautiful souls who were gentle when I was a child.

John Masefield

. . . Even for the least division of an hour
Have I been so beguiled as to be blind

To my most grievous loss? – That thought's return
Was the worst pang that sorrow ever bore
Save one, one only, when I stood forlorn,

Knowing my heart's best treasure was no more;
That neither present time, nor years unborn
Could to my sight that heavenly face restore.

                                        William Wordsworth

Wild Dreams of Summer What is Your Grief

Wild dreams of Summer, what is your grief?
Wild dreams of Winter, what is your delight?
O holy day, O holy day, so brief
O holy day, before so long a night.

My love, my love, no, there is no waking
From that long bed or that sleep.
My love, my love, the heart is here for the taking,
And we can take, but not keep.

                                        George Barker

Make bitter weeping, and make passionate wailing, and let thy mourning be according to his desert, for a day or two, lest thou be evil spoken of: and so be comforted for thy sorrow. For of sorrow cometh death, and sorrow of heart will bow down the strength . . . Give not thy heart unto sorrow: put it away, remembering the last end: forget it not, for there is no returning again: him thou shalt not profit, and thou wilt hurt thyself. Remember the sentence upon him; for so also shall thine be; yesterday for me, and today for thee.

Ecclesiasticus, 38

Epitaph

Even such is Time, which takes in trust
Our youth, our joys, and all we have,
And pays us but with age and dust;
Who in the dark and silent grave,
When we have wandered all our ways,
Shuts up the story of our days:
And from which earth, and grave, and dust,
The Lord shall raise me up, I trust.

Sir Walter Raleigh

An Epitaph

I was, I am not; smiled, that since did weep;
Laboured, that rest; I waked, that now must sleep;
I played, I play not; sung, that now am still;
Saw, that am blind; I would, that have no will;
I fed that which feeds worms; I stood, I fell;
I bade God save you, that now bid farewell;
I felt, I feel not; followed, was pursued;
I warred, have peace; I conquered, am subdued;
I moved, want motion; I was stiff, that bow
Below the earth; then something, nothing now;
I catched, am caught; I travelled, here I lie;
Lived in the world, that to the world now die.

Thomas Heywood

We are never better or freer from cares than when we sleep, and yet, which we so much avoid and lament, death is but a perpetual sleep; and why should it, as Epicurus argues, so much affright us? When we are, death is not: but when death is, then we are not: our life is tedious and troublesome unto him that lives best; ''tis a misery to be born, a pain to live, a trouble to die:' death makes an end of our miseries, and yet we cannot consider it; a little before Socrates drank his portion of cicuta, he bid the citizens of Athens cheerfully farewell, and concluded his speech with this short sentence; 'My time is now come to be gone. I to my death, you to live on; but which of these is best, God alone knows.'

...I am discontented, and why should I desire so much to live? But a happy death will make an end of all our woes and miseries; why shouldst not thou then say with old Simeon, since thou art so well affected. 'Lord, now let thy servant depart in peace;' Or with Paul, 'I desire to be dissolved and to be with Christ? 'tis a blessed hour that leads us to a blessed life, and blessed are they that die in the Lord.' . . . So likewise for our friends, why should their departure so much trouble us? They are better as we hope; and for what then dost thou lament, as those do whom Paul taxed in his time 'that have no hope'? . . . as Plutarch holds, 'Tis not in our power now to lament, it takes away mercy and pity not to be sad; 'tis a natural passion to weep for our friends, an irresistible passion to lament and grieve. . . .

From Robert Burton's *Anatomy of Melancholy*

Oh, if you did delight no more to stay
    Upon this low and earthly stage,
But rather chose an endless heritage,
Tell us at least we pray,
Where all the beauties that those ashes owed
Are now bestowed? . . .
Tell us, for oracles must still ascend,
For those that crave them at your tomb:
Tell us, where are those beauties now become,
And what they now intend?
Tell us, alas, that cannot tell our grief,
Or hope relief.

From *Elegy Over a Tomb* by Lord Herbert of Cherbury

Vanity of vanities saith the Preacher, vanity of vanities; all is vanity.

What profit hath a man of all his labour which he taketh under the sun?

One generation passeth away, and another generation cometh: but the earth abideth for ever. . . .

The thing that hath been it is that which shall be; and that which is done is that which shall be done: and there is nothing new under the sun . . .

There is no remembrance of former things; neither shall there be any remembrance of things that are to come with those that come after. . . .

And I gave my heart to know wisdom, and to know madness and folly: I perceived that this is also vexation of spirit.

For in much wisdom is much grief: and he that increaseth knowledge increaseth sorrow.

from Ecclesiastes 1. ii–xviii

A man should feel confident concerning his soul, who has renounced those pleasures and fineries that go with the body as being alien to him, and considering them to result more in harm than in good, but has pursued the pleasures that go with learning and made the soul fine with no alien but rather its own proper refinements, moderation and justice and courage and freedom and truth; thus it is ready for the journey to the world below.

Plato

'It was too perfect to last,' so I am tempted to say of our marriage. But it can be meant in two ways. It may be grimly pessimistic – as if God no sooner saw two of His creatures happy than He stopped it ('None of that here!'). As if He were like the Hostess at the sherry-party who separates two guests the moment they show signs of having got into a real conservation. But it could also mean 'This had reached its proper perfection. This had become what it had in it to be. Therefore of course it would not be prolonged.' As if God said, 'Good, you have mastered that exercise. I am very pleased with it. And now you are ready to go on to the next.' When you have learned to do quadratics and enjoy doing them you will not be set them much longer. The teacher moves you on.

For we did learn and achieve something. There is, hidden or flaunted, a sword between the sexes till an entire marriage reconciles them. It is arrogance in us to call frankness, fairness, and chivalry 'masculine' when we see them in a woman; it is arrogance in them to describe a man's senitiveness or tact or tenderness as 'feminine'. But also what poor, warped fragments of humanity most mere men and mere women must be to make the implications of that arrogance plausible. Marriage heals this. Jointly the two become fully human. 'In the image of God created he *them*.' Thus, by a paradox, this carnival of sexuality leads us out beyond our sexes.

And then one or other dies. And we think of this as love cut short; like a dance stopped in mid career or a flower with its head unluckily snapped off – something truncated and therefore, lacking its due shape. I wonder. If, as I can't help suspecting, the dead also feel the pains of separation (and this may be one of their purgatorial sufferings), then for both lovers, and for all pairs of lovers without exception, bereavement is a universal and integral part of our experience of love. It follows marriage as normally as marriage follows courtship or as autumn follows summer. It is not a truncation of the process but one of its phases; not the interruption of the dance, but the next figure. We are 'taken out of ourselves' by the loved one while she is here. Then comes the tragic figure of the dance in which we must learn to be still taken out of ourselves though the bodily presence is withdrawn, to love the very Her, and not fall back to loving our past, or our memory, or our sorrow, or our relief from sorrow, or our own love.

C. S. Lewis, *A Grief Observed*

C. S. Lewis to Owen Barfield on the Death of Charles Williams
18 May 1945

It has been a very odd experience. This, the first really severe loss I have suffered has (a) given a corroboration to my belief in immortality such as I never dreamed of – it is almost tangible now; (b) swept away all my old feelings of mere horror and disgust at funerals, coffins, graves, etc. – if need had been I think I could have handled *that* corpse with hardly any unpleasant sensations; (c) greatly reduced my feelings about ghosts. I think (but who knows?) that I should be, though afraid, more pleased than afraid if his turned up . . . To put it in a nutshell, what the idea of death has done to him is nothing to what he had done to the idea of death. Hit it for six; yet it used to rank as a fast bowler!

Messmates

He gave us all a good-bye cheerily
    At the first dawn of day;
We dropped him down the side full drearily
    When the light died away.
It's a dead dark watch that he's a-keeping there,
And a long, long night that lags a-creeping there
Where the Trades and the tides roll over him
    And the great ships go by.

He's there alone with green seas rocking him
    For a thousand miles round;
He's there alone with dumb things mocking him,
    And we're homeward bound.
It's a long, lone watch that he's a-keeping there,
And a dead cold night that lags a-creeping there,
While the months and the years roll over him,
    And the great ships go by.

I wonder if the tramps come near enough,
    As they thrash to and fro,
And the battleship's bells ring clear enough
    To be heard down below;
If through all the lone watch that he's a-keeping there,
And the long, cold night that lags a-creeping there,
The voices of the sailor-men shall comfort him
    When the great ships go by.

                                        Henry Newbolt

Sybylla's Dirge

We do lie beneath the grass
    In the moonlight, in the shade
Of the yew-tree. They that pass
    Hear us not. We are afraid
        They would envy our delight,
        In our graves by glow-worm night.
Come follow us, and smile as we;
    We sail to the rock in the ancient waves,
Where the snow falls by thousands into the sea,
    And the drowned and the shipwrecked have happy
            graves.

Thomas L. Beddoes

An Epitaph

Here lies a most beautiful lady,
Light of step and heart was she;
I think she was the most beautiful lady
That ever was in the West Country.
But beauty vanishes; beauty passes;
However rare, rare it be;
And when I crumble, who will remember
This lady of the West Country?

Walter de la Mare

Song

When I am dead, my dearest,
    Sing no sad songs for me;
Plant thou no roses at my head,
    Nor shady cypress tree:
Be the green grass above me
    With showers and dewdrops wet;
And if thou wilt, remember,
    And if thou wilt, forget.

I shall not see the shadows,
    I shall not feel the rain;
I shall not hear the nightingale
    Sing on, as if in pain;
And dreaming through the twilight
    That doth not rise nor set,
Haply I may remember,
    And haply may forget.

Christina Rosetti

Remember

Remember me when I am gone away,
    Gone far away into the silent land;
    When you can no more hold me by the hand,
Nor I half turn to go yet turning stay.
Remember me when no more day by day
    You tell me of our future that you planned:
    Only remember me; you understand

It will be late to counsel then or pray.
Yet if you should forget me for a while
    And afterwards remember, do not grieve:
    For if the darkness and corruption leave
    A vestige of the thoughts that once I had,
Better by far you should forget and smile
    Than that you should remember and be sad.

                         Christina Rosetti

But there are moments which he calls his own,
Then, never less alone than when alone,
Those whom he loved so long and sees no more,
Loved and still loves – not dead – but gone before,
He gathers round him.

                         Samuel Rogers

A Letter

Dear Friends
               Winter has come here.
It is not too bad as yet, though the darkness
Takes the centre, takes over, is beginning to make
Other things vague and futile. It
Is not all bad; the trees
Are sometimes very beautiful, it's just

It's sad that Summer has left us. It's more difficult
To get done the things expected of us. That apart,
It suits me in a way. Perhaps
The slowness in the blood begins to suit me.
It lets you out – Winter – and I feel so lazy.
What can you do but let things go, in Winter?
I write these things to you in another country
Lest in fine weather you should sorrow for me
And wish me in another place. I soon will be;
Like you in a climate untouched by the seasons
Except in people's minds. The dead are unreached
By any of our changes and yet we think
Of you as minding that we think of you,
As bathed in sunlight, comforted by air.
I write to you, dear Friends, to let you know
That I am all right here, knowing often
Love and glad things I wouldn't have elsewhere
But turning, really, longing sometimes so strong
For my quittance, my papers, my number to come up
And set off for your country.
                              See you soon.

                                        Jenny Joseph

In vain to me the smiling mornings shine,
    And redd'ning Phoebus lifts his golden fire;
The birds in vain their amorous descant join,
    Or cheerful fields resume their green attire:
These ears alas! for other notes repine,
    A different object do these eyes require.

My lonely anguish melts no heart but mine;
    And in my breast the imperfect joys expire.
Yet morning smiles the busy race to cheer,
    And new-born pleasure brings to happier men;
The fields to all their wonted tribute bear;
    To warm their little loves the birds complain.
I fruitless mourn to him that cannot hear,
    And weep the more because I weep in vain.

Thomas Gray, *On the Death of Richard West*

Remembrance

Cold in the earth – and the deep snow piled above thee!
Far, far removed, cold in the dreary grave!
Have I forgot, my Only Love, to love thee,
Severed at last by Time's all-severing wave?

Now, when alone, do my thoughts no longer hover
Over the mountains, on that northern shore,
Resting their wings were heath and fern-leaves cover
Thy noble heart for ever, ever more?

Cold in the earth, and fifteen wild Decembers
From those brown hills, have melted into spring –
Faithful indeed is the spirit that remembers
After such years of change and suffering!

Sweet Love of youth, forgive, if I forget thee,
While the World's tide is bearing me along:
Other desires and other hopes beset me,
Hopes which obscure but cannot do thee wrong.

No later light has lightened up my heaven,
No second morn has ever shone for me,
All my life's bliss from thy dear life was given –
All my life's bliss is in the grave with thee.

But when the days of golden dreams had perished
And even Despair was powerless to destroy,
Then did I learn how existence could be cherished
Strengthened and fed without the aid of joy;

Then did I check the tears of useless passion,
Weaned my young soul from yearning after thine;
Sternly denied its burning wish to hasten
Down to that tomb already more than mine!

And even yet, I dare not let it languish,
Dare not indulge in Memory's rapturous pain;
Once drinking deep of that divinest anguish,
How could I seek the empty world again?

                                        Emily Brontë

One Night

One night he lay on my breast,
One rapt swift-fleeting night;
Then marched away with the rest
In the morning light:
For I was only a woman, and so
I had to let him go.

And now another's breast
Holds him through endless night;
And he marches no more with the rest
In the morning light:
For she is his mother, the earth, and so
Need never let him go.

                                                    Wilfrid Gibson

Lament

We who are left, how shall we look again
Happily on the sun or feel the rain,
Without remembering how they who went
Ungrudgingly, and spent
Their all for us, loved too the sun and rain?

A bird among the rain-wet lilac sings –
But we, how shall we turn to little things,
And listen to the birds and winds and streams
Made holy by their dreams,
Nor feel the heart-break in the heart of things?

                                                    Wilfred Gibson

All Being Well

All being well, I'll come to you,
Sweetheart, before the year is through;
And we shall find so much to do,
So much to tell.

I read your letter through and through,
And dreamt of all we'd say and do,
Till in my heart the thought of you
Rang like a bell.

Now the bell tolls, my love, for you;
For long before the year is through
You've gone where there is naught to do
And naught to tell.

Yet mayn't I find when life is through
The best is still to say and do,
When I at last may come to you,
All being well?

                                    Wilfred Gibson

Poem

Heart of the heartless world,
Dear heart, the thought of you
Is the pain at my side,
The shadow that chills my view.

The wind rises in the evening
Reminds that autumn is near.
I am afraid to lose you,
I am afraid of my fear.

On the last mile to Huesca,
The last fence for our pride,
Think so kindly, dear, that I
Sense you at my side.

And if bad luck should lay my strength
Into the shallow grave,
Remember all the good you can;
Don't forget my love.

John Cornford

Perhaps –
(To R.A.L. Died of Wounds in France, December 23rd, 1915)

Perhaps some day the sun will shine again,
    And I shall see that still the skies are blue,
And feel once more I do not live in vain,
    Although bereft of You.

Perhaps the golden meadows at my feet
    Will make the sunny hours of Spring seem gay,
And I shall find the white May blossoms sweet,
    Though You have passed away.

Perhaps the summer woods will shimmer bright,
    And crimson roses once again be fair,
And autumn harvest fields a rich delight,
    Although You are not there.

Perhaps some day I shall not shrink in pain
    To see the passing of the dying year,
And listen to the Christmas songs again,
    Although You cannot hear.

But, though kind Time may many joys renew,
    There is one greatest joy I shall not know
Again, because my heart for loss of You
    Was broken, long ago.

                    1st London General Hospital, February 1916
                                            Vera Brittain

To My Brother
(In Memory of July 1st, 1916)

Your battle-wounds are scars upon my heart,
    Received when in that grand and tragic 'show'
You played your part
    Two years ago,

And silver in the summer morning sun
    I see the symbol of your courage glow –
That Cross you won
    Two years ago.

Though now again you watch the shrapnel fly,
    And hear the guns that daily louder grow,
As in July
    Two years ago,

May endure to lead the Last Advance
    And with your men pursue the flying foe
As once in France
    Two years ago.

                                        Vera Brittain

    Sleep on, my Love, in thy cold bed
Never to be disquieted.
My last good night! Thou wilt not wake
Till I thy fate shall overtake:
Till age, or grief, or sickness must
Marry my body to that dust
It so much loves; and fill the room
My heart keeps empty in thy tomb.
Stay for me there: I will not fail
To meet thee in that hollow vale.
And think not much of my delay;
I am already on the way,
And follow thee with all the speed
Desire can make, or sorrows breed.
Each minute is a short degree
And every hour a step towards thee.
At night when I betake to rest,
Next morn I rise nearer my west

Of life, almost by eight hours sail
Than when sleep breathed his drowsy gale.
    Thus from the sun my bottom steers,
And my day's compass downward bears.
Nor labour I to stem the tide
Through which to thee I swiftly glide.
    'Tis true, with shame and grief I yield;
Thou, like the van first took'st the field
And gotten hast the victory
In thus adventuring to die
Before me, whose more years might crave
A just precedence in the grave.
But hark! my pulse, like a soft drum,
Beats my approach, tells thee I come;
And slow howe'er my marches be
I shall at last sit down by thee.
    The thought of this bids me go on
And wait my dissolution
With hope and comfort. Dear, (forgive
The crime) I am content to live
Divided, with but half a heart,
Till we shall meet and never part.

                           Henry King

A Lamentation

All looks be pale, hearts cold as stone,
For Hally now is dead and gone.
        Hally in whose sight,
            Most sweet sight,
All the earth late took delight.
        Every eye, weep with me,
            Joys drowned in tears must be.

His ivory skin, his comely hair,
His rosy cheeks so clear and fair,
        Eyes that once did grace
            His bright face,
Now in him all want their place.
        Eyes and hearts, weep with me,
            For who so kind as he?

His youth was like an April flower,
Adorned with beauty, love and power.
        Glory strewed his way,
            Whose wreaths gay
Now all are turnèd to decay.
        Then, again, weep with me,
            None feel more cause than we.

No more may his wished sight return.
His golden lamp no more can burn,
        Quenched is all his flame,
            His hoped fame
Now hath left him nought but name.
        For him all weep with me,
            Since more him none shall see.

Thomas Campion

Joyce Grenfell to Lavinia Dyer on the
Death of her Husband Rex
Chelsea, 1975

Dear Lavinia,

Diana Lydon told me your tragic news and I write to send my thoughts and my real sympathy. I think perhaps there is an affinity between those who know what a good marriage is and my own ... fills me with compassion for you at this sad time. I don't know how you feel about it but I am increasingly sure that life is spiritual and therefore continuous – not in any spiritualistic way (material) but as the actual fact of our being, and because I believe this I'm sure that prayer which says 'Death is an horizon and our horizon is but the limitation of our view' is the truth.

We can *never* lose anything that is good never lose love or the memories of great happiness because they are *true*. I've come to the conclusion that only the eternal is real! And that means qualities that one loves in people – their humour, generosity, honour, kindness, gentleness etc. *are* the reality: and can never die. They are the identity of the one one loves.

I just felt I wanted to write to send you my thoughts and feeling and affection.

    Yours,
      Joyce Grenfell

Weep no more, woeful shepherds, weep no more,
For Lycidas, your sorrow, is not dead,
Sunk though he be beneath the watery floor;
So sinks the day-star in the ocean bed,
And yet anon repairs his drooping head,
And tricks his beams, and with new-spangled ore
Flames in the forehead of the morning sky:
So Lycidas sunk low, but mounted high,
Through the dear might of him that walked the waves,
Where, other groves and other streams along,
With nectar pure his oozy locks he laves,
And hears the unexpressive nuptial song,
In the blest kingdoms meek of joy and love.
There entertain him all the saints above,
In solemn troops and sweet societies,
That sing, and singing in their glory move,
And wipe the tears for ever from his eyes.
Now, Lycidas, the shepherds weep no more;
Henceforth thou art the Genius of the shore,
In thy large recompense, and shalt be good
To all that wander in that perilous flood.

John Milton: from *Lycidas*

He has outsoared the shadow of our night;
Envy and calumny and hate and pain,
And that unrest which men miscall delight,
Can touch him not and torture not again;
From the contagion of the world's slow stain
He is secure, and now can never mourn
A heart grown cold, a head grown gray in vain;
Nor, when the spirit's self has ceased to burn,
With sparkless ashes load an unlamented urn.

He is made one with Nature: there is heard
His voice in all her music, from the moan
Of thunder, to the song of night's sweet bird;
He is a presence to be felt and known
In darkness and in light, from herb and stone,
Spreading itself where'er that Power may move
Which has withdrawn his being to its own;
Which wields the world with never-wearied love,
Sustains it from beneath, and kindles it above.

                    *   *   *

The One remains, the many change and pass;
Heaven's light forever shines, Earth's shadows fly;
Life, like a dome of many-coloured glass,
Stains the white radiance of Eternity,
Until Death tramples it to fragments. – Die,
If thou wouldst be with that which thou dost seek!
Follow where all is fled! – Rome's azure sky,
Flowers, ruins, statues, music, works, are weak
The glory they transfuse with fitting truth to speak.

That light whose smile kindles the Universe,
That Beauty in which all things work and move,
That Benediction which the eclipsing Curse
Of birth can quench not, that sustaining Love
Which through the web of being blindly wove
By man and beast and earth and air and sea,
Burns bright or dim, as each are mirrors of
The fire for which all thirst; now beams on me,
Consuming the last clouds of cold mortality.

The breath whose might I have invoked in song
Descends on me; my spirit's bark is driven,
Far from the shore, far from the trembling throng
Whose sails were never to the tempest given;
The massy earth and spherèd skies are riven!
I am borne darkly, fearfully, afar;
Whilst, burning through the inmost veil of Heaven,
The soul of Adonais, like a star,
Beacons from the abode where the Eternal are.

P. B. Shelley
From 'Adonais'.

On My Late Dear Wife

(i)

Adieu, dear life! here am I left alone;
The world is strangely changed since thou art gone.
Compose thyself to rest, all will be well;
I'll come to bed 'as fast as possible'.

(ii)

Slumb'ring disturbed, appeared the well-known face,
Lovely, engaging, as she ever was;
I kissed and caught the phantom in my arms,
I knew it such, but such a shade hath charms!
Devout, I thanked kind heaven that, with a wife,
Had brightened up my choicest years of life;
But now, alas! 'tis thus! – She sighed – Poor heart!
A melancholy phantom as thou art,
From thee more happiness I thus receive
Than all the living woman-kind can give.
    This as I was about to say,
    But scrupling, is my heart yet free?
    It is, as on our wedding day,
    For she was all the sex to me.
I waked, and found it was a shade indeed.
She and her future sighs, or smiles, were fled;
I now am sighing in my widowed bed.

(iii)

I know not where, but gloomy was the place,
Methought I saw a gloomy phantom pass;
'Twas she, the much-loved form! nor spoke, nor stayed,
No motion of her eyes, or hand, or head,
But, gliding on, I lost her in the shade.
All solemn was, no argument of love
Appeared her inward sentiment to prove.
Confused and grieved, I stood; then spoke my heart:
Who could have thought such lovers thus would part!

(iv)

On My Dreaming of My Wife

As waked from sleep, methought I heard the voice
Of one that mourned; I listened to the noise.
I looked, and quickly found it was my dear,
Dead as she was, I little thought her there.
I questioned her with tenderness, while she
Sighed only, but would else still silent be.
I waked indeed; the lovely mourner's gone,
She sighs no more, 'tis I that sigh alone.

Musing on her, I slept again, but where
I went I know not, but I found her there.
Her lovely eyes she kindly fixed on me,
'Let Miser not be nangry then,' said she,
A language love had taught, and love alone
Could teach; we prattled as we oft had done,
But she, I know not how, was quickly gone.

With her imaginary presence blessed,
My slumbers are emphatically rest;
I of my waking thoughts can little boast,
They always sadly tell me she is lost.
Much of our happiness we always owe
To error, better to believe than know!
Return, delusion sweet, and oft return!
I joy, mistaken; undeceived, I mourn;
But all my sighs and griefs are fully paid,
When I but see the shadow of her shade.

Jonathan Richardson

On His Dead Wife

Methought I saw my late espousèd saint
   Brought to me like Alcestis from the grave,
   Whom Jove's great son to her glad husband gave,
   Rescued from death by force, though pale and faint.
Mine, as whom washed from spot of childbed taint
   Purification in the old Law did save,
   And such as yet once more I trust to have
   Full sight of her in heaven without restraint,
Came vested all in white, pure as her mind.
   Her face was veiled, yet to my fancied sight
   Love, sweetness, goodness, in her person shined
So clear as in no face with more delight.
   But O as to embrace me she inclined,
   I waked, she fled, and day brought back my night.

                           John Milton

From 'A Poem Written on His Brother's Death'

   O what a vanity is man!
How like the eye's quick wink
His cottage fails, whose narrow span
Begins even at the brink!
Nine months thy hands are fashioning us,
And many years (alas!)
Ere we can lisp, or ought discuss
Concerning Thee, must pass;

Yet have I known Thy slightest things,
A *feather* or a *shell*,
A stick, or rod which some chance brings,
The best of us excel.
    Yea, I have known these shreds outlast
  A fair-compacted frame,
And for one *twenty* we have past
Almost outlive our name.
    Thus hast Thou plac'd in man's outside
  Death to the common eye,
That Heaven within him might abide,
    And close Eternity.

Henry Vaughan

Surprised by joy – impatient as the wind
  I turned to share the transport – Oh! with whom
  But thee, deep buried in the silent tomb,
That spot which no vicissitude can find?
Love, faithful love, recalled thee to my mind –
  But how could I forget thee? Through what power,
  Even for the least division of an hour,
Have I been so beguiled as to be blind
To my most grievous loss! – That thought's return
  Was the worst pang that sorrow ever bore,
Save one, one only, when I stood forlorn,
  Knowing my heart's best treasure was no more;
That neither present time, nor years unborn
  Could to my sight that heavenly face restore.

William Wordsworth

A Reminiscence

Yes, thou art gone! and never more
   Thy sunny smile shall gladden me;
But I may pass the old church door,
   And pace the floor that covers thee,

May stand upon the cold, damp stone,
   And think that, frozen, lies below
The lightest heart that I have known,
   The kindest I shall ever know.

Yet, though I cannot see thee more,
   'Tis still a comfort to have seen;
And though thy transient life is o'er,
   'Tis sweet to think that thou hast been;

To think a soul so near divine,
   Within a form so angel fair,
United to a heart like thine,
   Has gladdened once our humble sphere.

Anne Brontë

Blows the wind to-day, and the sun and the rain are
    flying
  Blows the wind on the moors to-day and now
Where about the graves of the martyrs the whaups are
    crying
  My heart remembers how!

Grey recumbent tombs of the dead in desert places
   Standing stones on the vacant wine-red moor
Hills of sheep, and the howes of the silent vanished races
   And winds, austere and pure:

Be it granted me to behold you again in dying
   Hills of home! and to hear again the call;
Hear about the graves of the martyrs the peewees
    crying
   And hear no more at all.

R. L. Stevenson

She wrapped me round like a cloak, to keep all the hard and cold world off me. When I came home sick with mankind, there she was on the sofa, always with a cheerful story of something or somebody, and I never knew that she, poor darling, had been fighting with bitter pains all day.

To think that little dog should have been the instrument to take the light of life away from me! What would it be for me now to have the fame of Trismegistus, without her to be glad at it?

She never had a mean thought or word from the day I first saw her, looking like a flower out of the window of her mother's old brick house, my Jeanie, my queen.

Thomas Carlyle to Lord Houghton

Heraclitus

They told me. Heraclitus, they told me you were dead,
They brought me bitter news to hear and bitter tears to
    shed.
I wept as I remembered how often you and I
Had tired the sun with talking and sent him down the
    sky.

And now that thou art lying, my dear old Carian guest,
A handful of grey ashes, long, long ago at rest,
Still are they pleasant voices, thy nightingales, awake;
For Death, he taketh all away, but them he cannot take.

                           W. J. Cory

The Going

Why did you give no hint that night
That quickly after the morrow's dawn,
And calmly, as if indifferent quite,
You would close your term here, up and be gone
        Where I could not follow
        With wing of swallow
To gain one glimpse of you ever anon!

        Never to bid good-bye,
        Or lip me the softest call,
Or utter a wish for a word, while I
Saw morning harden upon the wall,
        Unmoved, unknowing
        That your great going
Had place that moment, and altered all.

Why do you make me leave the house
And think for a breath it is you I see
At the end of the alley of bending boughs
Where so often at dusk you used to be;
       Till in darkening dankness
       The yawning blankness
Of the perspective sickens me!

       You were she who abode
       By those red-veined rocks far West,
You were the swan-necked one who rode
Along the beetling Beeny Crest,
       And, reining nigh me,
       Would muse and eye me,
While Life unrolled us its very best.

Why, then, latterly did we not speak,
Did we not think of those days long dead,
And ere your vanishing strive to seek
That time's renewal? We might have said,
       'In this bright spring weather
       We'll visit together
Those places that once we visited.'

       Well, well? All's past amend
       Unchangeable. It must go.
I seem but a dead man held on end
To sink down soon. . . . O you could not know
       That such swift fleeing
       No soul foreseeing –
Not even I – would undo me so!

                          Thomas Hardy

Requiescat

Strew on her roses, roses,
  And never a spray of yew!
In quiet she reposes;
  Ah, would that I did too!

Her mirth the world required;
  She bathed it in smiles of glee.
But her heart was tired, tired,
  And now they let her be.

Her life was turning, turning,
  In mazes of heat and sound.
But for peace her soul was yearning,
  And now peace laps her round.

Her cabined, ample spirit,
  It fluttered and failed for breath.
To-night it doth inherit
  To vasty hall of death.

                                    Matthew Arnold

When Chuang Tzu's wife died, Hui Tzu came to the house to join in the rites of mourning. To his surprise he found Chuang Tzu sitting with an inverted bowl on his knees, drumming upon it and singing a song. 'After all,' said Hui Tzu, 'she lived with you, brought up your children, grew old along with you. That you should not mourn for her is bad enough; but to let your friends find you drumming and singing – that is going too far!' 'You misjudge me,' said Chuang Tzu. 'When she died, I was in despair, as any man well might be. But soon, pondering on what had happened, I told myself that in death no strange new fate befalls us. In the beginning we lack not life only, but form. Not form only, but spirit. We are blended in the one great featureless indistinguishable mass. Then a time came when the mass evolved spirit, spirit evolved form, form evolved life. And now life in its turn has evolved death. For not nature only but man's being has its seasons, its sequence of spring and autumn, summer and winter. If some one is tired and has gone to lie down, we do not pursue him with shouting and bawling. She whom I have lost has lain down to sleep for a while in the Great Inner Room. To break in upon her rest with the noise of lamentation would but show that I knew nothing of nature's Sovereign Law. That is why I ceased to mourn.'

Arthur Waley, *Three Ways of Thought in Ancient China*

For a Gentle Friend

I have come to where the deep words are
Spoken with care. There is no more to hide.
I toss away the cold stance of my fear

And move far, far out to be beside
One who owns all language in extremes
Of death. We watch the coming-in now tide.

We have lived through the nightmares death presumes
To wound us with. We faced the darkest place.
Death the familiar enters all our rooms.

We wear its colour. Its mask's on our face.
But not for long. It's good to let tears run.
This is the quick, the nerve, also the grace

Of death. It brings our life into the sun
And we are grateful. Grief is gracious when
It takes the character of this kind one,

This gentle person. We re-live his life
And marvel at the quiet good he's done.

                                    Elizabeth Jennings

Darkness and light divide the course of time, and oblivion
shares with memory a great part even of our living
beings: we slightly remember our felicities, and even the
smartest strokes of affliction leave but short smart upon
us. Sense endureth no extremities, and sorrows destroy
us or themselves. To weep into stones are fables.
Afflictions induce callosities; miseries are slippery, or fall
like snow upon us, which notwithstanding is no unhappy
stupidity. To be ignorant of evils to come and forgetful
of evils past, is a merciful provision in nature whereby
we digest the mixture of our few and evil days, and, our
delivered senses not relapsing into cutting remembrances,
our sorrows are not kept raw by the edge of repetitions.
A great part of antiquity contented their hopes of

subsistency with a transmigration of their souls: a good way to continue their memories while having the advantage of plural successions, they could not but act something remarkable in such a variety of beings, and enjoining the fame of their past selves, make accumulation of glory unto their last durations. Others, rather than be lost in the uncomfortable night of nothing, were content to recede into the common being, and make one particle of the public soul of all things, which was no more than to return into their unknown and divine origin again. Egyptian ingenuity was more unsatisfied, contriving their bodies in sweet consistencies, to attend the return of their soul. But all was vanity, feeding the wind, and folly.

Sir Thomas Browne: from *Urn Burial*

If parting of friends, absence alone, can work such violent effects, what shall death do, when they must be eternally separated, never in this world to meet again? This is so grievous torment for the time, that it takes away their appetite, desire of life, extinguisheth all delights, it causeth deep sighs and groans, tears, exclamations, howling, roaring, many bitter pangs and by frequent meditation extends so far sometimes, they think that they see their dead friends continually in their eyes. . . . 'still, still, still, that good father, that good son, that good wife, that dear friend,' runs in their minds: all all the year long, as Pliny complains to Romanus 'methinks I see Virginius, I hear Virginius, I talk with Virginius.' They that are most staid and patient, are so furiously carried headlong by the

passion of sorrow in this case that brave discreet men
otherwise, oftentimes forget themselves, and weep like
children many months together, 'as if they to water
would', and will not be comforted. 'They are gone; they
are gone; what shall I do? . . .'

. . . 'Rachel wept for her children, and would not be
comforted because they were not.' So did Adrian the
emperor bewail his Antinous; Hercules Hylas; Orpheus
Eurydice; David Absalom; Austin his mother Monica,
Niobe her children, insomuch that the poets feigned her
to be turned into a stone, as being stupified through the
extremity of grief . . .

Robert Burton: *Anatomy of Melancholy*

In thinking of all these virtues hold again, as it were,
your son in your arms! He has now more leisure to
devote to you, there is nothing now to call him away
from you; never again will he cause you anxiety, never
again any grief. The only sorrow you could possibly
have had from a son so good is the sorrow you have had;
all else is now exempt from the power of chance, and
holds nought but pleasure if only you know how to
enjoy your son, if only you come to understand what his
truest value was. Only the image of your son – and a
very imperfect likeness it was – has perished; he himself
is eternal and has reached now a far better state, stripped
of all outward encumbrances and left simply himself . . .

Seneca, *Ad Marciam de Consolatione,* tr. J. W. Basore

On the Death of His Father

I look up and see his curtains and bed:
I look down and examine his table and mat.
The things are there just as before.
But the man they belonged to is not there.
His spirit suddenly has taken flight
And left me behind far away.
To whom shall I look on whom rely?
My tears flow in an endless stream.
'Yu, yu' cry the wandering deer
As they carry fodder to their young in the wood.
Flap, flap fly the birds
As they carry their little ones back to the nest.
I alone am desolate
Dreading the days of our long parting:
My grieving heart's settled pain
No one else can understand.
There is a saying among people
'Sorrow makes us grow old.'
Alas, alas for my white hairs!
All too early they have come!
Long wailing, long sighing
My thoughts are fixed on my sage parent.
They say the good live long:
Then why was *he* not spared?

Wei Wēn-ti, translated by Arthur Waley

But for sorrow there is no remedy provided by nature; it is often occasioned by accidents irreparable, and dwells upon objects that have lost or changed their existence; it requires what it cannot hope, that the laws of the universe should be repealed; that the dead should return, or the past should be recalled.

Sorrow is not that regret for negligence or error which may animate us to future care or activity, or that repentance of crimes for which, however irrevocable, our Creator has promised to accept it as an atonement; the pain which arises from these causes has very salutary effects and is every hour extenuating itself by the reparation of those miscarriages that produce it. Sorrow is properly that state of mind in which our desires are fixed upon the past, without looking forward to the future, an incessant wish that something were otherwise than it has been, a tormenting and harassing want of some enjoyment or possession which we have lost, and which no endeavours can possibly regain. Into such anguish many have sunk upon some sudden diminution of their fortune, an unexpected blast of their reputation, or the loss of children or of friends. They have suffered all sensibility of pleasure to be destroyed by a single blow, have given up for ever the hopes of substituting any other object in the room of that which they lament, resigned their lives to gloom and despondency, and worn themselves out in unavailing misery.

Yet so much is this passion the natural consequences of tenderness and endearment, that however painful and however useless, it is justly reproachful not to feel it on some occasions; and so widely and constantly has it always prevailed, that the laws of some nations, and the customs of others, have limited a time for the external appearances of grief caused by the dissolution of close aliances, and the breach of domestick union.

It seems determined by the general suffrage of mankind, that sorrow is to a certain point laudable, as the offspring of love, or at least pardonable as the effect of weakness; but that it ought not to be suffered to increase by indulgence, but must give way after a stated time to social duties, and the common avocations of life. It is at first unavoidable, and therefore must be allowed, whether with or without our choice; it may afterwards be admitted as a decent and affectionate testimony of kindness and esteem; something will be extorted by nature, and something may be given to the world. But all beyond the bursts of passion, or the forms of solemnity, is not only useless but culpable; for we have no right to sacrifice, to the vain longings of affection, that time which Providence allows us for the task of our station. . . .

. . . Sorrow is a kind of rust of the soul, which every new idea contributes in its passage to scour away. It is the putrefaction of stagnant life, and is remedied by exercise and motion.

Samuel Johnson: from *The Rambler*

How Sleep the Brave

How sleep the brave, who sink to rest
By all their country's wishes blest!
When Spring, with dewy fingers cold,
Returns to deck their hallowed mould,
She there shall dress a sweeter sod
Than Fancy's feet have ever trod.

By fairy hands their knell is rung,
By forms unseen their dirge is sung;
There Honour comes, a pilgrim grey,
To bless the turf that wraps their clay,
And Freedom shall awhile repair
To dwell a weeping hermit there!

William Collins

Epitaph on a Soldier

His body lies interred within this mould,
Who died a young man yet departed old;
And in all strength of youth that man can have
Was ready still to drop into his grave:
For aged in virtue, with a youthful eye
He welcomed it, being still prepared to die,
And living so, though young deprived of breath,
He did not suffer an untimely death;
But we may say of his brave blest decease –
He died in war, and yet he died in peace.

Cyril Tourneur, *The Atheist's Tragedy*

Elegy

O snatch'd away in beauty's bloom!
On thee shall press no ponderous tomb;
But on thy turf shall roses rear
Their leaves, the earliest of the year,
And the wild cypress wave in tender gloom:

And oft by yon blue gushing stream
Shall Sorrow lean her drooping head,
And feed deep thought with many a dream,
And lingering pause and lightly tread;
Fond wretch! as if her step disturb'd the dead!

Away! we know that tears are vain,
That Death nor heeds nor hears distress:
Will this unteach us to complain?
Or make one mourner weep the less?
And thou, who tell'st me to forget,
Thy looks are wan, thine eyes are wet.

Byron

Lelant
(In memory of Thomasine Trenoweth, aged 23)

The little meadow by the sand,
Where Tamsin lies, is ringed about
With acres of the scented thyme.
The salt wind blows in all that land;

The great clouds pace across the skies;
Rare wanderers from the ferry climb.
One might sleep well enough, no doubt,
    Where Tamsin lies.

Tamsin has sunshine now and wind,
And all in life she might not have,
The silence and the utter peace
That tempest-winnowed spirits find
On slopes that front the western wave.
The white gulls circle without cease
    O'er Tamsin's grave.

E. K. Chambers

Room for a Soldier! lay him in the clover;
He loved the fields, and they shall be his cover;
Make his mound with hers who called him once her
    lover:
    Where the rain may rain upon it,
    Where the sun may shine upon it,
    Where the lamb hath lain upon it,
    And the bee will dine upon it.

Bear him to no dismal tomb under city churches;
Take him to the fragrant fields, by the silver birches,
Where the whippoorwill shall mourn, where the oriole
    perches:
    Make his mound with sunshine on it.

Thomas William Parsons, The Magnolia

A Leave-Taking

Let us go hence, my songs; she will not hear.
Let us go hence together without fear;
Keep silence now, for singing-time is over,
And over all old things and all things dear.
She loves not you nor me as we all love her.
Yea, though we sang as angels in her ear,
    She would not hear.

Let us rise up and part; she will not know.
Let us go seaward as the great winds go,
Full of blown sand and foam; what help is here?
There is no help, for all these things are so,
And all the world is bitter as a tear.
And how these things are, though ye strove to show,
    She would not know.

Let us go home and hence; she will not weep.
We gave love many dreams and days to keep,
Flowers without scent, and fruits that would not grow,
Saying, 'If thou wilt, thrust in thy sickle and reap.'
All is reaped now; no grass is left to mow;
And we that sowed, though all we fell on sleep,
    She would not weep.

Let us go hence and rest; she will not love.
She shall not hear us if we sing hereof,
Nor see love's ways, how sore they are and steep.
Come hence, let be, lie still; it is enough.
Love is a barren sea, bitter and deep;
And though she saw all heaven in flower above,
    She would not love.

Let us give up, go down; she will not care.
Though all the stars made gold of all the air,
And the sea moving saw before it move
One moon-flower making all the foam-flowers fair;
Though all those waves went over us, and drove
Deep down the stifling lips and drowning hair,
        She would not care.

Let us go hence, go hence; she will not see.
Sing all once more together; surely she,
She too, remembering days and words that were,
Will turn a little towards us, sighing; but we,
We are hence, we are gone, as though we had not been
        there.
Nay, and though all men seeing had pity on me,
        She would not see.

                                        A. C. Swinburne

A Letter from Charlotte Brontë
about the death of her sister Emily

'Some sad comfort I take, as I hear the wind blow and
feel the cutting keenness of the frost, in knowing that the
elements bring her no more suffering; their severity
cannot reach her grave; her fever is quieted, her
restlessness soothed, her deep hollow cough is hushed for
ever; we do not hear it in the night nor listen for it in
the morning.; we have not the conflict of the strangely
strong spirit and the fragile frame before us – relentless
conflict – once seen, never forgotten . . . I will not now

ask why Emily was torn from us in the fulness of our attachment, rooted up in the prime of her own days, in the promise of her powers; why her existence now lies like a field of green corn trodden down, like a tree in full bearing struck at the root. I will only say, sweet is rest after labour and calm after tempest, and repeat again and again that Emily knows that now.'

Elegy Written in a Country Churchyard

The curfew tolls the knell of parting day,
The lowing herd wind slowly o'er the lea,
The ploughman homeward plods his weary way,
And leaves the world to darkness and to me.

Now fades the glimmering landscape on the sight,
And all the air a solemn stillness holds,
Save where the beetle wheels his droning flight,
And drowsy tinklings lull the distant folds;

Save that from yonder ivy-mantled tower
The moping owl does to the moon complain
Of such as, wandering near her secret bower,
Molest her ancient solitary reign.

Beneath those rugged elms, that yew-tree's shade,
Where heaves the turf in many a mouldering heap,
Each in his narrow cell for ever laid,
The rude forefathers of the hamlet sleep.

The breezy call of incense-breathing morn,
The swallow twittering from the straw-built shed,
The cock's shrill clarion or the echoing horn,
No more shall rouse them from their lowly bed.

For them no more the blazing hearth shall burn,
Or busy housewife ply her evening care:
No children run to lisp their sire's return,
Or climb his knees the envied kiss to share.

Oft did the harvest to their sickle yield,
Their furrow oft the stubborn glebe has broke;
How jocund did they drive their team afield!
How bowed the woods beneath their sturdy stroke!

Let not Ambition mock their useful toil,
Their homely joys and destiny obscure;
Nor Grandeur hear, with a disdainful smile,
The short and simple annals of the poor.

The boast of heraldry, the pomp of power,
And all that beauty, all that wealth e'er gave,
Awaits alike the inevitable hour.
The paths of glory lead but to the grave.

Nor you, ye Proud, impute to these the fault,
If Memory o'er their tomb no trophies raise,
Where through the long-drawn aisle and fretted vault
The pealing anthem swells the note of praise.

Can storied urn or animated bust
Back to its mansion call the fleeting breath?
Can Honour's voice provoke the silent dust,
Or Flattery soothe the dull cold ear of Death? . . .

Full many a gem of purest ray serene
The dark unfathomed caves of ocean bear:
Full many a flower is born to blush unseen,
And waste its sweetness on the desert air.

Some village-Hampden that with dauntless breast
The little tyrant of his fields withstood;
Some mute inglorious Milton here may rest,
Some Cromwell guiltless of his country's blood. . . .

Far from the madding crowd's ignoble strife
Their sober wishes never learned to stray;
Along the cool sequestered vale of life
They kept the noiseless tenor of their way. . . .

                              Thomas Gray, from his *Elegy*

Strong Son of God, immortal Love,
        Whom we, that have not seen thy face,
        By faith, and faith alone, embrace,
Believing where we cannot prove;

Thine are these orbs of light and shade;
        Thou madest Life in man and brute;
        Thou madest Death; and lo, thy foot
Is on the skull which thou hast made.

Thou wilt not leave us in the dust:
        Thou madest man, he knows not why;
        He thinks he was not made to die;
And thou hast made him: thou art just.

Thou seemest human and divine,
        The highest, holiest manhood, thou:
        Our wills are ours, we know not how;
Or wills are ours, to make them thine.

Our little systems have their day;
        They have their day and cease to be:
        They are but broken lights of thee,
And thou, O Lord, art more than they.

We have but faith: we cannot know;
        For knowledge is of things we see;
        And yet we trust it comes from thee,
A beam in darkness: let it grow.

Let knowledge grow from more to more,
        But more of reverence in us dwell;
        That mind and soul, according well,
May make one music as before,

But vaster. We are fools and slight;
        We mock thee when we do not fear:
        But help thy foolish ones to bear;
Help thy vain worlds to bear thy light.

Forgive what seem'd my sin in me;
        What seem'd my worth since I began;
        For merit lives from man to man,
And not from man, O Lord, to thee.

Forgive my grief for one removed,
        Thy creature, whom I found so fair.
        I trust he lives in thee, and there
I find him worthier to be loved.

Forgive these wild and wandering cries,
> Confusions of a wasted youth;
> Forgive them where they fail in truth,
And in thy wisdom make me wise.

Alfred, Lord Tennyson, from *In Memoriam.*

And thou art dead, as young and fair
As aught of mortal birth;
And forms so soft and charms so rare
Too soon return'd to Earth!
Though Earth received them in her bed,
And o'er the spot the crowd may tread
In carelessness or mirth,
There is an eye which could not brook
A moment on that grave to look. . . .

Yet did I love thee to the last,
As fervently as thou
Who didst not change through all the past
And canst not alter now.
The love where Death has set his seal
Nor age can chill, nor rival steal,
Nor falsehood disavow:
And, what were worse, thou canst not see
Or wrong, or change, or fault in me. . . .

I know not if I could have borne
To see thy beauties fade;
The night that follow'd such a morn
Had worn a deeper shade:

Thy day without a cloud hath past,
And thou wert lovely to the last,
Extinguish'd, not decay'd;
As stars that shoot along the sky
Shine brightest as they fall from high. . . .

Yet how much less it were to gain,
Though thou hast left me free,
The loveliest things that still remain
Than thus remember thee!
The all of thine that cannot die
Though dark and dread Eternity
Returns again to me,
And more thy buried love endears
Than aught except its living years.

Byron: from *Elegy to Thyrza*

Here rests his head upon the lap of earth
A youth to fortune and to fame unknown.
Fair Science frowned not on his humble birth,
And Melancholy marked him for her own.

Large was his bounty and his soul sincere,
Heaven did a recompense as largely send:
He gave to Mis'ry all he had, a tear,
He gained from heav'n ('twas all he wished) a friend.

No farther seek his merits to disclose,
Or draw his frailties from their dread abode
(There they alike in trembling hope repose),
The bosom of his Father and his God.

Thomas Gray: The Epitaph to his *Elegy*

6

Classical Translations

It is true of the body, is it not? that physical evil, namely disease, wastes and destroys it until it is no longer a body at all, and all the other things we instanced are annihilated by the pervading corruption of the evil which peculiarly besets them. Now is it true in the same way of the soul that injustice and other forms of vice, by besetting and pervading it, waste it away in corruption until they sever it from the body and bring about its death?

No, certainly not . . .

For if its own evil and depravity cannot kill the soul, it is hardly likely that an evil designed for the destruction of a different thing will destroy the soul or anything but its own proper object. So, since the soul is not destroyed by any evil, either its own or another's, clearly it must be a thing that exists for ever, and is consequently immortal.

Plato, *The Republic*, translated F. M. Cornford

Other translations from Classical Authors are to be found on pages 1, 7, 108–109, 120, 153, 238, 239, 248–9, 261–2, 277 (translation of Lucretius), 345, 346 and 347.

So death, the most terrifying of ills, is nothing to us, since so long as we exist, death is not with us; but when death comes, then we do not exist. It does not then concern either the living or the dead, since for the former it is not, and the latter are no more.

Epicurus, *Letter to Menoeceus*, translated Cyril Bailey

Alone of gods Death has no love for gifts,
Libation helps you not, nor sacrifice.
He has no altar, and he hears no hymns;
From him alone Persuasion stands apart.

Aeschylus, *Niobe*, translated C. M. Bowra

Some have said that bees possess a share of the divine mind, and draw the breath of heaven; for they think that the deity moves through all lands and open spaces of the sea, and deep of heaven; that hence flocks, herds, men, every kind of wild beast, each one at birth, derive the delicate spirit of life; and so, in course, all things are restored to this fountain, and thither return again by dissolution; and there is no room for death, but each flies up into the place of a star, and climbs the height of heaven.

Virgil

Prudentius
The Burial of the Dead

Take him, earth, for cherishing,
    To thy tender breast receive him.
Body of a man I bring thee,
    Noble even in its ruin.

Once was this a spirit's dwelling,
    By the breath of God created.
High the heart that here was beating,
    Christ the prince of all its living.

Guard him well, the dead I give thee,
    Not unmindful of His creature
Shall he ask it: he who made it
    Symbol of his mystery.

Comes the hour God hath appointed
    To fulfil the hope of men,
Then must thou, in very fashion,
    What I give, return again.

Not though ancient time decaying
    Wear away these bones to sand,
Ashes that a man might measure
    In the hollow of his hand:

Not though wandering winds and idle,
    Drifting through the empty sky,
Scatter dust was nerve and sinew,
    Is it given man to die.

Once again the shining road
    Leads to ample Paradise;
Open are the woods again
    That the Serpent lost for men.

Take, O take him, mighty Leader,
　　Take again thy servant's soul,
To the house from which he wandered
　　Exiled, erring, long ago.

But for us, heap earth about him,
　　Earth with leaves and violets strewn,
Grave his name, and pour the fragrant
　　Balm upon the icy stone.

　　　　　　　　　　　　　Translated H. Waddell

When a man has such things to think on, and sees the
Sun, the Moon, and stars, and enjoys Earth and Sun, he is
not solitary or even helpless.

　　What else can I do, a lame old man, but sing hymns to
God? If then I were a nightingale, I would do the
nightingale's part; if I were a swan, I would do as a swan.
But now I am a rational creature and I ought to praise
God. This is my work; I do it, nor will I desert my post
so long as I am allowed to keep it; and I exhort you to
join in this same song.

　　　　　　　　　　　　　Epictetus the Slave

The Morning Star

Thou wert the morning star among the living,
  Ere thy fair light had fled;
Now, having died, thou art as Hesperus, giving
  New splendour to the dead.

From Plato, translated by Shelley

Nothing that is extreme is evil. Death comes to you? It would be dreadful could it remain with you; but of necessity either it does not arrive or else it departs.

Seneca, *Letters to Lucilius*

7

I Jewish and Christian

To every thing there is a season, and a time to every purpose under the heaven.

A time to be born and a time to die; a time to plant and a time to pluck up that which is planted;

A time to kill and a time to heal; a time to break down and a time to build up.

A time to weep and a time to laugh; a time to mourn and a time to dance.

A time to get and a time to lose; a time to keep and a time to cast away.

A time to rend and a time to sew; a time to keep silence, and a time to speak.

A time to love and a time to hate; a time of war, and a time of peace.

For that which befalleth the sons of men befalleth beasts; even one thing befalleth them: as the one dieth, so dieth the other; yea, they have all the breath; so that a man hath no preeminence above a beast: for all is vanity.

Ecclesiastes, Chapter 3

For to him that is joined to all the living there is hope: for a living dog is better than a dead lion. For the living know that they shall die: but the dead know not any thing, neither have they any more a reward; for the memory of them is forgotten. Also their love, and their hatred, and their envy, is now perished; neither have they any more a portion for ever in any thing that is done under the sun.

Ecclesiastes, Chapter 9

The days of our age are threescore years and ten: and though men be so strong, that they come to fourscore years: yet is their strength then but labour and sorrow; so soon passeth it away, and we are gone.

But who regardeth the power of thy wrath: for even thereafter as a man feareth, so is thy displeasure.

So teach us to number our days: that we may apply our hearts unto wisdom.

Turn thee again, O Lord, at the last: and be gracious unto thy servants.

O satisfy us with thy mercy, and that soon: so shall we rejoice and be glad all the days of our life.

Comfort us again now after the time that thou hast plagued us: and for the years wherein we have suffered adversity.

Shew thy servants thy work: and their children thy glory.

And the glorious Majesty of the Lord our God be upon us: prosper thou the work of our hands upon us, O prosper thou our handy-work.

Book of Common Prayer (1662)

Let us now praise famous men, and our fathers that begat us. The Lord hath wrought great glory by them through his great power from the beginning. Such as did bear rule in their kingdoms, men renowned for their power, giving counsel by their understanding, and declaring prophecies: leaders of the people by their counsels, and by their knowledge of learning meet for the people, wise and eloquent in their instructions: such as found out musical tunes, and recited verses in writing: rich men furnished with ability, living peaceably in their habitations: all these were honoured in their generations, and were the glory of their times. There be of them, that have left a name behind them, that their praises might be reported. And some there be, which have no memorial; who are perished, as though they had never been; and are become as though they had never been born; and their children after them. But these were merciful men, whose righteousness hath not been forgotten. With their seed shall continually remain a good inheritance, and their children are within the covenant. Their seed standeth fast, and their children for their sakes. Their seed shall remain for ever, and their glory shall not be blotted out. Their bodies are buried in peace; but their name liveth for evermore. The people will tell of their wisdom, and the congregation will shew forth their praise.

Ecclesiasticus 44: 1-15

Nothing is here for tears, nothing to wail
Or knock the breast; no weakness, no contempt,
Dispraise or blame; nothing but well and fair,
And what may quiet us in a death so noble.

John Milton: Samson Agonistes

Out of my Soul's Depth

Out of my soul's depth to thee my cries have sounded:
Let thine ears my plaints receive, on just fear grounded.
Lord, shouldst thou weigh our faults, who's not
      confounded?

But with grace thou censur'st thine when they have
      erred,
Therefore shall they blessed name be lov'd and feared.
Ev'n to thy throne my thoughts and eyes are reared.

Thee alone my hopes attend, on thee relying;
In thy sacred word I'll trust, to thee fast flying,
Long ere the watch shall break, the morn descrying.

In the mercies of our God who live secured,
May of full redemption rest in him assured,
Their sin-sick souls by him shall be recured.

Thomas Campion

Twenty-Third Psalm

The Lord is my shepherd; I shall not want.

He maketh me to lie down in green pastures: he leadeth me beside the still waters.

He restoreth my soul: he leadeth me in the paths of righteousness for his name's sake.

Yea, though I walk through the valley of the shadow of death, I will fear no evil, for thou art with me; thy rod and thy staff they comfort me.

Thou preparest a table before me in the presence of mine enemies: thou anointest my head with oil; my cup runneth over.

Surely goodness and mercy shall follow me all the days of my life, and I will dwell in the house of the Lord for ever.

Jerusalem, my happy home,
  When shall I come to thee?
When shall my sorrows have an end?
  Thy joys when shall I see?

O happy harbour of the saints,
  O sweet and pleasant soil!
In thee no sorrow may be found,
  No grief, no care, no toil.

No dampish mist is seen in thee,
  Nor cold nor darksome night;
There every soul shines as the sun,
  There God himself gives light.

There lust and lucre cannot dwell,
    There envy bears no sway;
There is no hunger, heat nor cold,
    But pleasure every way.

Thy houses are of ivory,
    Thy windows crystal clear,
Thy tiles are made of beaten gold,
    O God, that I were there.

Within thy gates doth nothing come
    That is not passing clean;
No spider's web, no dirt, no dust,
    No filth may there be seen.

Thy gardens and thy gallant walks
    Continually are green;
There grows such sweet and pleasant flowers
    As nowhere else are seen.

Jerusalem, my happy home,
    Would God I were in thee!
Would God my woes were at an end,
    Thy joys that I might see!

                                            Anon

O God, our help in ages past,
    Our hope for years to come,
A shelter from the stormy blast,
    And our eternal home;

Beneath the shadow of thy throne
    Thy saints have dwelt secure;
Sufficient is thine arm alone,
    And our defence is sure.

Before the hills in order stood,
And earth received her frame,
From everlasting thou art God,
For endless years the same.

A thousand ages in thy sight
    Are like an evening gone;
Short as the watch that ends the night
    Before the rising sun.

Time, like an ever-rolling stream,
    Bears all its sons away;
They fly forgotten, as a dream
    Dies at the opening day.

O God, our help in ages past,
    Our hope for years to come,
Be thou our guard while troubles last,
    And our eternal home.

Isaac Watts

Set me as a seal upon thine heart, as a seal upon thine arm: for love is strong as death; jealousy is cruel as the grave: the coals thereof are coals of fire, which hath a most vehement flame.

Many waters cannot quench love, neither can the floods drown it: if a man would give all the substance of his house for love, it would utterly be contemned.

Song of Solomon, 8

David's Lament for Jonathan

The beauty of Israel is slain upon thy high places: how are the mighty fallen!

Tell it not in Gath, publish it not in the streets of Askelon, lest the daughters of the Philistines rejoice.

Ye mountains of Gilboa, let there be no dew, neither let there be rain upon you, nor fields of offerings, for there the shield of the mighty is cast away, the shield of Saul.

From the blood of the slain, from the fat of the mighty, the bow of Jonathan turned not back, and the sword of Saul returned not empty.

Saul and Jonathan were lovely and pleasant in their lives, and in their death they were not divided: they were swifter than eagles, they were stronger than lions.

Ye daughters of Israel, weep over Saul, who clothed you in scarlet, with other delights, who put ornaments of gold on your apparel.

How are the mighty fallen in the midst of the battle!

O Jonathan, thou wast slain in thine high places.

I am distressed for thee, my brother Jonathan. Very pleasant hast thou been unto me; thy love to me was wonderful, passing the love of women.

How are the mighty fallen, and the weapons of war perished!

1 Samuel

David's Lament for Absalom

David sat between the two gates; and the watchman went up to the roof and lifted up his eyes, and looked, and behold a man running alone. The watchman cried, and told the king; and the king said, If he be alone, there is tidings in his mouth. And he came apace, and drew near.

And, behold, Cushi came, and said, Tidings, my lord the king, for the Lord hath avenged thee this day of all them that rose up against thee. And the king said, Is the young man Absalom safe? And Cushi answered, The enemies of my lord the king, and all that rise against thee to do thee hurt, be as that young man is.

And the king was much moved, and went up to the chamber over the gate, and wept; and as he went he said, *O my son Absalom! my son, my son Absalom! Would God I had died for thee, O Absalom, my son, my son!*

It was told Joab, *Behold, the king weepeth and mourneth for Absalom*; and the victory that day was turned into mourning unto all the people, for the people heard how the king was grieved for his son. And the people gat them by stealth into the city, as people being ashamed steal away when they flee in battle.

But the king covered his face, and cried with a loud voice, *O my son Absalom! O Absalom, my son, my son!*

2 Samuel

'God doth not say, live well and thou shalt die well, that is, an easie, a quiet death; But live well here, and thou shalt live well for ever. As the first part of a sentence peeces well with the last, and never respects, never hearkens after the parenthesiss that comes betweene, so doth a good life here flowe into an eternall life, without any consideration, what manner of death wee dye: But whether the gate of my prison be opened with an oyld key (by a gentle and preparing sickness) or the gate bee hewen downe by a violent death, or the gate bee burnt downe by a raging and frantique fever, a gate into heaven I shall have, for from the Lord is the cause of my life, and with God the Lord are the issues of death. And further wee cary not this second acceptation of the words, as this issue of death is *liberatio in morte*, God's care that the soule be safe, what agonies soever the body suffers in the hours of death . . .'

John Donne

They shall awake as Jacob did, and say as Jacob said, Surely the Lord is in this place, and this is no other but the house of God, and the gate of heaven, And into that gate they shall enter, and in that house they shall dwell, where there shall be no Cloud nor Sun, no darkness nor dazzling, but one equal light, no noise nor silence, but one equal music, no fears nor hopes, but one equal possession, no foes nor friends, but one equal communion and Identity, no ends nor beginnings, but one equal eternity.

John Donne

We brought nothing into this world, and it is certain we can carry nothing out. The Lord gave, and the Lord hath taken away; blessed be the Name of the Lord.

1 Tim. 6.7. Job 1.21. *Prayer Book*

Light Shining out of Darkness

God moves in a mysterious way,
   His wonders to perform;
He plants his footsteps in the sea,
   And rides upon the storm.

Deep in unfathomable mines
    Of never failing skill
He treasures up his bright designs,
    And works his sovereign will.

Ye fearful saints, fresh courage take,
    The clouds ye so much dread
Are big with mercy, and shall break
    In blessings on your head.

Judge not the Lord by feeble sense,
    But trust him for his grace;
Behind a frowning providence,
    He hides a smiling face.

His purposes will ripen fast,
    Unfolding every hour;
The bud may have a bitter taste,
    But sweet will be the flower.

Blind unbelief is sure to err,
    And scan his work in vain;
God is his own interpreter,
    And he will make it plain.

                                    William Cowper

I am now ready to be offered, and the time of my departure is at hand. I have fought a good fight; I have finished my course; I have kept the faith: henceforth there is laid up for me a crown of righteousness, which the Lord, the righteous judge, shall give me at that day, and not to me only, but unto all them that love his appearing.

Paul to Timothy

What reason do atheists have to say that one cannot rise from the dead? Which is the more difficult, to be born or to be reborn? That that which has never existed should exist, or that that which has existed should exist again? Is it more difficult to come into being than to return to it? Custom makes the one seem easy, absence of custom makes the other seem impossible: a vulgar way of judging!

Pascal, *Pensées*

Extracts from the Funeral Sermon for Lady Carbery

There is no age of man but it hath proper to itself some posterns and out-lets for death, besides those infinite and open ports out of which myriads of men and women every day pass into the dark, and the land of forgetfulness.

Infancy hath life but *in effigie*, or like a spark dwelling in
a pile of wood: the candle is so newly lighted, that every
little shaking of the taper, and every ruder breath of air
puts it out, and it dies. Childhood is so tender, and yet so
unwary; so soft to all the impressions of chance, and yet
so forward to run into them, that God knew there could
be no security without the care and vigilance of an angel-
keeper: and the eyes of parents and the arms of nurses,
the provisions of art, and all the effects of human love
and providence, are not sufficient to keep one child from
horrid mischiefs, from strange and early calamities and
deaths, unless a messenger be sent from heaven to stand
sentinel, and watch the very playings and sleepings, the
eatings and drinkings of the children; and it is a long
time before nature makes them capable of help: for there
are many deaths, and very many diseases to which poor
babes are exposed; but they have but very few capacities
of physic: to shew that infancy is as liable to death as old
age, and equally exposed to danger, and equally uncapable
of a remedy: with this only difference, that old age hath
diseases incurable by nature, and the diseases of childhood
are incurable by art: and both the states are the next heirs
of death.

Men live in their course and by turns; their light
burns a while, and then it burns blue and faint, and men
go to converse with spirits, and then they reach the taper
to another; and as the hours of yesterday can never
return again, so neither can the man whose hours they
were, and who lived them over once, he shall never
come to live them again, and live them better.

. . . But then we should do well also to remember that in
this world we are something besides flesh and blood;
that we may not without violent necessities run into

new relations, but preserve the affections we bore to our dead when they were alive. We must not so live as if they were perished, but so as pressing forward to the most intimate participation of the communion of saints. And we also have some ways to express this relation, and to bear a part in this communion, by actions of intercourse with them, and yet proper to our state: such as are, strictly performing the will of the dead, providing for, and tenderly and wisely educating their children, paying their debts, imitating their good example, preserving their memories privately, and publicly keeping their memorials, and desiring of God with hearty and constant prayer that God would give them a joyful resurrection, and a merciful judgment, (for so S. Paul prayed in behalf of Onesiphorus,) that 'God would shew them mercy in that day,' that fearful, and yet much to be desired day, in which the most righteous person hath need of much mercy and pity, and shall find it. Now these instances of duty shew that the relation remains still; and though the relict of a man or woman hath liberty to contract new relations, yet I do not find they have liberty to cast off the old, as if there were no such thing as immortality of souls. Remember that we shall converse together again; let us therefore never do any thing of reference to them which we shall be ashamed of in the day when all secrets shall be discovered, and that we shall meet again in the presence of God: in the mean time, God watcheth concerning all their interest, and He will in His time both discover and recompense. For though, as to us, they are like water spilt; yet to God they are as water fallen into the sea, safe and united in His comprehension and inclosures . . .

. . . God will restore the soul to the body, and raise the body to such a perfection that it shall be an organ fit to praise Him upon; it shall be made spiritual to minister to the soul, when the soul is turned into a spirit; then the soul shall be brought forth by angels from her incomparable and easy bed, from her rest in Christ's holy bosom, and be made perfect in her being, and in all her operations. And this shall first appear by that perfection which the soul shall receive as instrumental to the last judgment; for then she shall see clearly all the records of this world, all the register of her own memory. For all that we did in this life is laid up in our memories; and though dust and forgetfulness be drawn upon them, yet when God shall lift us from our dust, then shall appear clearly all that we have done, written in the tables of our conscience, which is the soul's memory.

Jeremy Taylor

In No Strange Land

O world invisible, we view thee,
O world intangible, we touch thee,
O world unknowable, we know thee,
Inapprehensible, we clutch thee!

Does the fish soar to find the ocean,
The eagle plunge to find the air—
That we ask of the stars in motion
If they have rumour of thee there?

Not where the wheeling systems darken,
And our benumbed conceiving soars!—
The drift of pinions, would we hearken,
Beats at our own clay-shuttered doors.

The angels keep their ancient places;—
Turn but a stone, and start a wing!
'Tis ye, 'tis your estangèd faces,
That miss the many-splendoured thing.

But (when so sad thou canst not sadder)
Cry;—and upon thy so sore loss
Shall shine the traffic of Jacob's ladder
Pitched betwixt Heaven and Charing Cross.

Yea, in the night, my Soul, my daughter,
Cry,—clinging Heaven by the hems;
And lo, Christ walking on the water,
Not of Gennesareth, but Thames!

                                        Francis Thompson

Heaven-Haven

I have desired to go
      Where springs not fail,
To fields where flies no sharp and sided hail
      And a few lilies blow.

And I have asked to be
      Where no storms come,
Where the green swell is in the havens dumb,
      And out of the swing of the sea.

                                  Gerard Manley Hopkins

I see my way as birds their trackless way.
I shall arrive! What time, what circuit first,
I ask not; but unless God sends His hail,
Or blinding fire balls, or sleet, or stifling snow,
In some good time—His good time—I shall arrive;
He guides me and the bird. In His good time!

Robert Browning

We cannot deceive God and nature; for a coffin is a
coffin, though it be covered with a pompous veil; and
the minutes of our time strike on and are counted by
Angels, till the period comes which must cause the
passing bell to give warning to all the neighbours that
thou art dead, and they must be so; and nothing can
excuse or retard this. And if our death could be put off a
little longer, what advantage can it be in thy accounts of
nature or felicity? They that 3,000 years agone died
unwillingly, and stopped death two days, or stayed a
week, what is their gain? *Where is that week?*

Jeremy Taylor, *Holy Being*

Virtue

Sweet day, so cool, so calm, so bright,
The bridal of the earth and sky:
The dew shall weep thy fall tonight,
                For thou must die.

Sweet rose, whose hue angry and brave
Bids the rash gazer wipe his eye:
Thy root is ever in its grave,
                And thou must die.

Sweet spring, full of sweet days and roses,
A box where sweets compacted lie:
My music shows ye have your closes,
                And all must die.

Only a sweet and virtuous soul,
Like seasoned timber never gives;
But though the whole world turn to coal,
                Then chiefly lives.

George Herbert

Give me my scallop-shell of Quiet;
My staff of Faith to walk upon;
My scrip of Joy, immortal diet;
My bottle of Salvation;
My gown of Glory, hope's true gage;
And thus I'll take my pilgrimage.
Blood must be my body's balmer,—
No other balm will there be given—
Whilst my soul, like a white palmer,
Travels to the land of Heaven;
Over the silver mountains,
Where spring the nectar fountains—
And there I'll kiss
The bowl of Bliss,
And drink my eternal fill
On every milken hill:
My soul will be a-dry before,
But after it will ne'er thirst more.

Sir Walter Raleigh
from *The Passionate Man's Pilgrimage*

Never weather-beaten sail more willing bent to shore,
Never tired pilgrim's limbs affected slumber more,
Than my wearied sprite now longs to fly out of my
    troubled breast;
O come quickly, sweetest Lord, and take my soul to rest!

Ever blooming are the joys of heaven's high Paradise,
Cold age deafs not there our ears nor vapour dims our
    eyes:
Glory there the sun outshines; whose beams the Blessëd
    only see
O come quickly, glorious Lord, and raise my sprite to
    Thee!

                                        Thomas Campion

Thou hast made me, and shall thy work decay?
    Repair me now, for now mine end doth haste;
    I run to death, and death meets me as fast,
And all my pleasures are like yesterday.
I dare not move my dim eyes any way;
    Despair behind, and death before doth cast
    Such terror, and my feebled flesh doth waste
By sin in it, which it towards hell doth weigh.
Only thou art above, and when towards thee
    By thy leave I can look, I rise again;
But our old subtle foe so tempteth me
    That not one hour I can myself sustain.
    Thy grace may wing me to prevent his art,
And thou like adamant draw mine iron heart.

                        John Donne: from *Holy Sonnets*

To leave unseen so many a glorious sight,
To leave so many lands unvisited,
To leave so many books unread,
Unrealized so many visions bright;—
Oh! wretched yet inevitable spite
Of our short span, and we must yield our breath,
And wrap us in the unfeeling coil of death,
So much remaining of unproved delight.
But hush, my soul, and vain regrets be still'd;
Find rest in Him Who is the complement
Of whatsoe'er transcends our mortal doom,
Of broken hope and frustrated intent;
In the clear vision and aspect of Whom
All wishes and all longings are fulfill'd.

R. C. Trench

We Thirst at First

We thirst at first—'tis nature's act
And later, when we die,
A little water supplicate
Of fingers going by.

It intimates the finer want
Whose adequate supply
Is that greater water in the west
Termed Immortality.

Emily Dickinson

When I bethinke me on that speech whyleare,
  Of Mutability, and well it way:
Me seemes, that though she all unworthy were
  Of the Heav'ns Rule; yet very sooth to say,
  In all things else she beares the greatest sway.
Which makes me loath this state of life so tickle,
  And love of things so vaine to cast away;
Whose flowring pride, so fading and so fickle,
Short Time shall soon cut down with his consuming
    sickle.

Then gin I thinke on that which Nature sayd,
  Of that same time when no more Change shall be,
But stedfast rest of all things firmely stayd
  Upon the pillours of Eternity,
  That is contrayr to Mutabilitie:
For, all that moveth, doth in Change delight:
  But thence-forth all shall rest eternally
With Him that is the God of Sabbaoth hight:
O that great Sabbaoth God, graunt me that Sabaoths
    sight.

  Edmund Spenser: from *Nature's Reply to Mutability*

And so our discussion went on. Suppose, we said, that
the tumult of a man's flesh were to cease and all that his
thoughts can conceive, of earth, of water, and of air,
should no longer speak to him; suppose that the heavens
and even his own soul were silent, no longer thinking of
itself but passing beyond; suppose that his dreams and
the visions of his imagination spoke no more and that

every tongue and every sign and all that is transient grew silent—for all these things have the same message to tell, if only we can hear it, and their message is this: We did not make ourselves, but he who abides for ever made us. Suppose, we said, that after giving us this message and bidding us listen to him who made them, they fell silent and he alone should speak to us, not through them but in his own voice, so that we should hear him speaking, not by any tongue of the flesh or by an angel's voice, not in the sound of thunder or in some veiled parable, but in his own voice, the voice of the one whom we love in all these created things; suppose that we heard him himself, with none of these things between ourselves and him, just as in that brief moment my mother and I had reached out in thought and touched the eternal Wisdom which abides over all things; suppose that this state were to continue and all other visions of things inferior were to be removed, so that this single vision entranced and absorbed the one who beheld it and enveloped him in inward joys in such a way that for him life was eternally the same as that instant of understanding for which we had longed so much—would not this be what we are to understand by the words *Come and share the joy of your Lord*? But when is it to be? Is it to be when *we all rise again, but not all of us will undergo the change*?

St Augustine: *Confessions*

Death is nothing at all . . . I have only slipped away into the next room. I am I and you are you. Whatever we were to each other that we are still. Call me by my old familiar name, speak to me in the easy way which you always used. Put no difference in your tone; wear no forced air of solemnity or sorrow. Laugh as we always laughed at the little jokes we enjoyed together. Play, smile, think of me, pray for me. Let my name be ever the household word that it always was. Let it be spoken without effort, without the ghost of a shadow on it. Life means all that it ever meant. It is the same as it ever was; there is absolutely unbroken continuity. Why should I be out of mind because I am out of sight? I am waiting for you for an interval, somewhere very near, just around the corner. All is well.

Henry Scott Holland

At the Burial of the Dead

Now is Christ risen from the dead, and become the first-fruits of them that slept. For since by man came death, by man came also the resurrection of the dead. For as in Adam all die, even so in Christ shall all be made alive. But every man in his own order: Christ the first-fruits; afterward they that are Christ's, at his coming. Then cometh the end, when he shall have delivered up the kingdom to God, even the Father; when he shall have put down all rule, and all authority, and power. For he must reign, till he hath put all enemies under his feet. The last enemy that shall be destroyed is death. For he hath put all things under his feet. But when he saith, all things are put under him, it is manifest that he is excepted, which did put all things under him. And when all things shall be subdued unto him, then shall the Son also himself be subject unto him that put all things under him, that God may be all in all. Else what shall they do which are baptized for the dead, if the dead rise not at all? Why are they then baptized for the dead? and why stand we in jeopardy every hour? I protest by your rejoicing, which I have in Christ Jesus our Lord, I die daily. If after the manner of men I have fought with beasts at Ephesus, what advantageth it me, if the dead rise not? Let us eat and drink, for to-morrow we die. Be not deceived: evil communications corrupt good manners. Awake to righteousness, and sin not; for some have not the knowledge of God. I speak this to your shame. But some man will say, How are the dead raised up? and with what body do they come? Thou fool, that which thou sowest is not quickened, except it die. And that which thou sowest, thou sowest not that body that shall be, but bare grain, it may chance of wheat, or of some other grain: But God giveth it a body, as it hath pleased him, and to every seed his own body. All flesh is not the same flesh; but there is one kind of flesh of men, another flesh of beasts, another of fishes, and another of birds. There are also celestial bodies, and bodies terrestrial; but the glory of the celestial is one, and the glory of the terrestrial is another. There is one glory of the sun, and another glory of the moon, and another glory of the stars; for one star differeth from another star in glory. So also is the resurrection of the dead: It is sown in corruption; it is raised in incorruption: It is sown in dishonour; it is raised in glory: It is sown in weakness; it is raised in power: It is sown a natural body; it is

raised a spiritual body. There is a natural body, and
there is a spiritual body. And so it is written, The first
man Adam was made a living soul; the last Adam was
made a quickening spirit. Howbeit that was not first
which is spiritual, but that which is natural; and
afterward that which is spiritual. The first man is of the
earth, earthy: the second man is the Lord from heaven.
As is the earthy, such are they that are earthy: and as is
the heavenly, such are they also that are heavenly. And
as we have borne the image of the earthy, we shall also
beat the image of the heavenly. Now this I say,
brethren, that flesh and blood cannot inherit the
kingdom of God; neither doth corruption inherit
incorruption. Behold, I shew you a mystery: We shall
not all sleep, but we shall all be changed, in a moment,
in the twinkling of an eye, at the last trump, (for the
trumpet shall sound,) and the dead shall be raised
incorruptible, and we shall be changed. For this
corruptible must put on incorruption, and this mortal
must put on immortality. So when this corruptible shall
have put on incorruption, and this mortal shall have put
on immortality; then shall be brought to pass the saying
that is written, Death is swallowed up in victory. O
death, where is thy sting? O grave, where is thy
victory? The sting of death is sin, and the strength of sin
is the law. But thanks be to God, which giveth us the
victory through our Lord Jesus Christ. Therefore, my
beloved brethren, be ye stedfast, unmoveable, always
abounding in the work of the Lord, forasmuch as ye
know that your labout is not in vain in the Lord.

The Book of Common Prayer (1662)
from I Corinthians 15:20

The immortality of the soul is a thing which concerns us so greatly and deeply, that a man must be lost to all feeling who can be indifferent as to the knowledge thereof. Every action and thought in life must needs take so various a course, according as there is an eternal good to be hoped for or not, that it is impossible to take any step with good sense and judgment, save as regulated with respect to this point, which must be our final object.

So our first interest and our first object is to be enlightened on this subject, whereon our whole conduct in life depends. And herein, among those who are not yet convinced, I place a wide interval between those who labour with all their energy to learn and those who live on without anxiety or thought for the matter.

I can feel nought but the tenderest compassion for those who mourn sincerely their doubt, who reckon it a heavy misfortune, and who, sparing no effort to come forth, make the search after truth their main and most earnest pursuit. . . .

. . . Nothing is so important to man as his actual state, nothing so awful as eternity. And therefore, if we find men who are indifferent to the loss of existence and to the risk of everlasting misery, it is altogether an unnatural state. They are quite different as to everything else; they fear the slightest evil, they foresee and are acutely sensitive to it; and the very same man who will spend days and nights in passionate despair at the loss of office, or at some fancied affront, will accept what to him is a fact—that he is about to lose everything by death, without anxiety or emotion. It is a marvellous perversion to see one identical heart so sensitive to trifles and so strangely callous to the weightiest matters. It is an incomprehensible delusion, a supernatural drowsiness, which betokens the influence of a mighty power.

Pascal: *Pensées* (transl. H. L. S. Lear)

From the Wisdom of Solomon

But the souls of the righteous are in the hand of God,
and there shall no torment touch them.

   In the sight of the unwise they seemed to die: and
their departure is taken for misery.

   And their going from us to be utter destruction: but
they are in peace. For though they be punished in the
sight of men, yet is their hope full of immortality.

   And having been a little chastised, they shall be
greatly rewarded: for God proved them, and found
them worthy for himself . . .

Lord, thou hast been our refuge : from one generation
to another.

   Before the mountains were brought forth, or ever
the earth and the world were made : thou art God from
everlasting, and world without end.

   Thou turnest man to destruction : again thou sayest,
Come again, ye children of men.

   For a thousand years in thy sight are but as yesterday:
seeing that is past as a watch in the night.

   As soon as thou scatterest them they are even as a
sleep : and fade away suddenly like the grass.

   In the morning it is green, and groweth up : but in
the evening it is cut down, dried up, and withered.

   For we consume away in thy displeasure : and are
afraid at thy wrathful indignation.

   Thou hast set our misdeeds before thee : and our
secret sins in the light of thy countenance.

For when thou art angry all our days are gone : we bring our years to an end, as it were a tale that is told.

The days of our age are threescore years and ten; and though men be so strong that they come to fourscore years : yet is their strength then but labour and sorrow; so soon passeth it away, and we are gone.

But who regardeth the power of thy wrath : for even thereafter as a man feareth, so is thy displeasure.

So teach us to number our days : that we may apply our hearts unto wisdom.

Turn thee again, O Lord, at the last : and be gracious unto thy servants.

O satisfy us with thy mercy, and that soon : so shall we rejoice and be glad all the days of our life.

Comfort us again now after the time that thou hast plagued us : and for the years wherein we have suffered adversity.

Shew thy servants thy work : and their children thy glory.

And the glorious Majesty of the Lord our God be upon us : prosper thou the work of our hands upon us, O prosper thou our handy-work.

Psalm 90

Who would True valour see,
Let him come hither;
One here will constant be,
Come Wind, come Weather.
There's no Discouragement

Shall make him once relent
His first avow'd intent
To be a Pilgrim.

Who so beset him round
With dismal Stories
Do but themselves confound,
His Strength the more is;
No Lion can him fright,
He'll with a Giant fight,
But he will have a right
To be a Pilgrim.

Hobgoblin nor foul Fiend
Can daunt his spirit;
He knows he at the end
Shall Life inherit.
Then Fancies fly away,
He'll fear not what men say.
He'll labour night and day
To be a Pilgrim.

John Bunyan

Then there came forth a Summons for Mr. Stand-fast (this Mr. Stand-fast was that he that the rest of the Pilgrims found upon his Knees in the Enchanted Ground), for the Post brought it him open in his hands. The contents whereof were, that he must prepare for a Change of Life, for his Master was not willing that he should be so far from him any longer. At this Mr. Stand-fast was put into a muse. Nay, said the Messenger, you need not doubt of the truth of my Message, for here is a

Token of the Truth thereof, Thy Wheel is broken at the Cistern. Then he called to him Mr. Great-heart who was their Guide, and said unto him, Sir, although it was not my hap to be much in your good Company in the days of my Pilgrimage, yet since the time I knew you, you have been profitable to me. When I came from home, I left behind me a Wife and five small Children, let me entreat you at your return (for I know that you will go and return to your Master's house, in hopes that you may yet be a Conductor to more of the holy Pilgrims), that you send to my Family, and let them be acquainted with all that hath and shall happen unto me. Tell them, moreover, of my happy Arrival to this place, and of the present late blessed condition that I am in. Tell them also of Christian and Christiana his Wife, and how she and her Children came after her Husband. Tell them also of what a happy end she made, and whither she is gone. I have little or nothing to send to my Family, except it be Prayers and Tears for them; of which it will suffice if thou acquaint them, if peradventure they may prevail.

When Mr. Stand-fast had thus set things in order, and the time being come for him to haste him away, he also went down to the River. Now there was a great Calm at that time in the River; wherefore Mr. Stand-fast, when he was about half-way in, stood a while, and talked to his Companions that had waited upon him thither. And he said:

This River has been a Terror to many, yea, the thoughts of it also have often frightened me. But now methinks I stand easy, my Foot is fixed upon that upon which the Feet of the Priests that bare the Ark of the Covenant stood while Israel went over this Jordan. The Waters indeed are to the Palate bitter and to the Stomach cold, yet the thoughts of what I am going to, and of the

Conduct that waits for me on the other side, doth lie as a glowing Coal at my Heart.

I see myself now at the end of my Journey, my toilsome days are ended. I am going now to see that Head that was crowned with Thorns, and that Face that was spit upon for me.

I have formerly lived by Hearsay and Faith, but now I go where I shall live by sight, and shall be with him in whose Company I delight myself.

I have loved to hear my Lord spoken of, and wherever I have seen the print of his Shoe in the Earth, there I have coveted to set my Foot too.

His name has been to me as a Civet-box, yea, sweeter than all Perfumes. His Voice to me has been most sweet, and his Countenance I have more desired than they that have most desired the Light of the Sun. His word I did use to gather for my Food, and for Antidotes against my Faintings. He has held me, and I have kept me from mine iniquities, yea, my Steps hath he strengthened in his Way.

Now while he was thus in Discourse, his Countenance changed, his strong man bowed under him, and after he had said, Take me, for I come unto thee, he ceased to be seen of them.

John Bunyan: from *The Pilgrim's Progress*

Now Mr. Despondency's Daughter, whose name was Much-afraid, said, when she heard what was done, that she would go with her Father. Then Mr. Despondency said to his Friends, Myself and my Daughter, you know what we have been, and how troublesomely we have

behaved ourselves in every Company. My Will and my
Daughter's is, that our Desponds and slavish Fears be by
no man ever received from the day of our Departure for
ever, for I know that after my Death they will offer
themselves to others. For, to be plain with you, they are
Ghosts, the which we entertained when we first began
to be Pilgrims, and could never shake them off after; and
they will walk about and seek entertainment of the
Pilgrims, but for our sakes shut ye the doors upon them.

When the time was come for them to depart, they
went to the Brink of the River. The last words of Mr.
Despondency were, Farewell Night, welcome Day. His
Daughter went through the River singing, but none
could understand what she said.

*   *   *

After this it was noised abroad that Mr. Valiant-for-
truth was taken with a Summons by the same Post as the
other, and had this for a Token that the Summons was
true, That his Pitcher was broken at the Fountain. When
he understood it, he called for his Friends, and told them
of it. Then said he, I am going to my Father's, and though
with great difficulty I am got hither, yet now I do not
repent me of all the Trouble I have been at to arrive
where I am. My Sword I give to him that shall succeed
me in my Pilgrimage, and my Courage and Skill to him
that can get it. My Marks and Scars I carry with me, to
be a witness for me that I have fought his Battles who
now will be my Rewarder. When the day that he must
go hence was come, many accompanied him to the
Riverside, into which as he went he said, Death, where is
thy Sting? And as he went down deeper he said, Grave,
where is thy Victory? So he passed over, and all the
Trumpets sounded for him on the other side.

John Bunyan: from *The Pilgrim's Progress*

II Buddhism, Hinduism and Zen

Questioner: What is death?

KRISHNAMURTI: You have seen dead bodies being carried to the river; you have seen dead leaves, dead trees; you know that fruits wither and decay. The birds that are so full of life in the morning, chattering away, calling to each other, by evening may be dead. The person who is alive today may be struck down by disaster tomorrow. We see all this going on. Death is common to us all. We will all end that way. You may live for thirty, fifty, or eighty years, enjoying, suffering, being fearful; and at the end of it you are no more.

What is it that we call living, and what is it that we call death? If we can find out, if we can understand what living is, then perhaps we shall understand what death is. When we lose someone whom we love, we feel bereft, lonely; therefore we say that death has nothing to do with living. We separate death from life. But is death separate from life? Is not living a process of dying?

Now, what is it that comes to an end in death? Is it life? What is life? Is life merely a process of breathing in air and expelling it? Eating, hating, loving, acquiring, possessing, comparing, being envious – this is what most of us know as life. For most of us life is suffering, a constant battle of pain and pleasure, hope and frustration. And can that not come to an end? Should we not die? In the autumn, with the coming of cold weather, the leaves fall from the trees, and reappear in the spring. Similarly, should we not die to everything of yesterday, to all our accumulations and hopes, to all the successes that we have gathered? Should we not die to all that and live again tomorrow, so that, like a new leaf, we are fresh, tender, sensitive? To a man who is constantly dying, there is no death. But the man who says, 'I am somebody and I must continue' – to him there is always death and the burning-ghat; and that man knows no love.

from *Krishnamurti* (Penguin selection)

Then Almitra spoke, saying, We would ask now of Death.

And he said:

You would know the secret of death.

But how shall you find it unless you seek it in the heart of life?

The owl whose night-bound eyes are blind unto the day cannot unveil the mystery of light.

If you would indeed behold the spirit of death, open your heart wide unto the body of life.

For life and death are one, even as the river and the sea are one.

In the depth of your hopes and desires lies your silent knowledge of the beyond;

And like seeds dreaming beneath the snow your heart dreams of spring.

Trust the dreams, for in them is hidden the gate to eternity.

Your fear of death is but the trembling of the shepherd when he stands before the kind whose hand is to be laid upon him in honour.

Is the shepherd not joyful beneath his trembling, that he shall wear the mark of the king?

Yet is he not more mindful of his trembling?

For what is it to die but to stand naked in the wind and to melt into the sun?

And what is it to cease breathing but to free the breath from its restless tides, that it may rise and expand and seek God unencumbered?

Only when you drink from the river of silence shall you indeed sing.

And when you have reached the mountain top, then you shall begin to climb.

And when the earth shall claim your limbs, then shall you truly dance.

K. Gibran: from *The Prophet*

Your essence was not born and will not die. It is neither being nor nonbeing. It is not a void nor does it have form. It experiences neither pleasure nor pain. If you ponder what it is in you that feels the pain of this sickness, and beyond that you do not think or desire or ask anything, and if your mind dissolves like vapour in the sky, then the path to rebirth is blocked and the moment of instant release has come.

Bassui, Zen Buddhist, comforting a dying person

A man acts according to the desires to which he clings. After death he goes to the next world bearing in mind the subtle impressions of his deeds; and, after reaping there the harvest of those deeds, he returns again to this world of action. Thus he who has desire continues subject to rebirth.

He who lacks discrimination, whose mind is unsteady and whose heart is impure, never reaches the goal, but is born again and again. But he who has discrimination, whose mind is steady and whose heart is pure, reaches the goal and, having reached it, is born no more.

Upanishads

Accept my homage, Earth, as I make my last obeisance
            of the day,
      Bowed at the altar of the setting sun.

You are mighty, and knowable only by the mighty;
      You counterpoise charm and severity;
            Compounded of male and female

You sway human life with unbearable conflict.
    The cup that your right hand fills with nectar
        Is smashed by your left;
   Your playground rings with your mocking laughter.
    You make herosim hard to attain;
       You make excellence costly;
You are not merciful to those who deserve mercy.
   Ceaseless warfare is hidden in your plants:
Their crops and fruits are victory-wreaths won from
          struggle.
    Land and sea are your cruel battlefields –
Life proclaims its triumph in the face of death.
Civilization rests its foundation upon your cruelty:
   Ruin is the penalty exacted for any shortcoming. . . .

   . . . At your footstool mounted on evil as well as
          good,
   To your vast and terrifying beauty,
  I offer today my scarred life's homage.
I touch your huge buried store of life and death,
    Feel it throughout my body and mind.
The corpses of numberless generations of men lie
        heaped in your dust:
I too shall add a few fistfuls, the final measure of my joys
        and pains:
   Add them to that name-absorbing, shape-absorbing,
        fame-absorbing
     Silent pile of dust. . . .

   . . . You are gentle and fierce, ancient and renewing;
    You emerged from the sacrificial fire of primal
        creation
      Immeasurably long ago.

Your cyclic pilgrimage is littered with meaningless
                remnants of history;
     You abandon your creations without regret; strew
                them layer upon layer;
          Forgotten.

     Guardian of Life, you nurture us
          In little cages of fragmented time,
     Boundaries to all our games, limits to all renown.

Today I stand before you without illusion:
     I do not ask at your door for immortality
          For the many days and nights I have spent
                weaving you garlands.
               But if I have given true value
     To my small seat in a tiny segment of one of the eras
          That open and close like blinks in the millions of
                years
               Of your solar round;
     If I have won from the trials of life a scrap of success;
          Then mark my brow with a sign made from your
                clay –
               To be rubbed out in time by the night
     In which all signs fade into the final unknown.

          O aloof, ruthless Earth,
               Before I am utterly forgotten
          Let me place my homage at your feet. . . .

Rabindranath Tagore: from *Earth* translated William Radice

It was my songs that taught me all the lessons I ever learnt; they showed me secret paths, they brought before my sight many a star on the horizon of my heart.

They guided me all day long to the mysteries of the country of pleasure and pain, and at last to what palace gate have they brought me in the evening at the end of my journey?

Rabindranath Tagore

There is a bridge between time and eternity; and this bridge is Atman, the Spirit of man. Neither day nor night cross that bridge, nor old age, nor death nor sorrow.

Evil or sin cannot cross that bridge, because the world of the Spirit is pure. This is why when this bridge has been crossed, the eyes of the blind can see, the wounds of the wounded are healed, and the sick man becomes whole from his sickness.

To one who goes over that bridge, the night becomes like unto day; because in the worlds of the Spirit there is a light which is everlasting.

Upanishads

It comes only in true awakening.
Fools strive after sanctity,
Or for rewards.
The stone lantern lifts its hand:
Daybreak is here.
The void smiles and
Nods its great head.

                                             Nensho

Life and Death

Suddenly light
Suddenly dark –
I am firefly too.

                                             Chinejo

The moon sinks
Behind the mountain.
Across the wide watery darkness
Fishing-lights wink.
We think we are alone but
Far out there on the midnight sea
Oars are splashing
A long way out,
Further out than us.

                                             Manyoshu

Life and Death

While living, identify with life; when dying, with death. Do not give way, do not desire. Life and death are the essential being of Buddha. If therefore you abandon life and death you will lose; and if you attach yourself either to life or to death, you will lose. Do not hate and do not desire; do not think and do not speak of these things. Forget your body and spirit and put them in the Buddha's hands and let him guide you. Then without striving for an end you will reach freedom and Buddhahood. The way there is easy. Shun evil, do nothing about life and death, show mercy to all living things, show respect to your superiors and sympathy to your inferiors. Do not like or dislike. Live without worry or speculation. That is the only way to Buddhahood.

Dogen

8

Mysticism and Pantheism

The corn was orient and immortal wheat, which never should be reaped, nor was ever sown. I thought it had stood from everlasting to everlasting. The dust and stones of the street were as precious as gold: the gates were at first the end of the world. The green trees when I saw them first through one of the gates transported and ravished me, their sweetness and unusual beauty made my heart to leap, and almost mad with ecstasy, they were such strange and wonderful things. The Men! O what venerable and reverend creatures did the aged seem! Immortal Cherubims! And young men glittering and sparkling Angels, and maids strange seraphic pieces of life and beauty! Boys and girls tumbling in the street, and playing, were moving jewels. I knew not that they were born or should die; But all things abided eternally as they were in their proper places. Eternity was manifest in the Light of the Day, and something infinite behind everything appeared: which talked with my expectation and moved my desire. The city seemed to stand in Eden, or to be built in Heaven. The streets were mine, the temple was mine, the people were mine, their clothes and gold and silver were mine, as much as their sparkling eyes, fair skins and ruddy faces. The skies were mine, and so were the sun and moon and stars, and all the World was mine; and I the only spectator and I enjoyer of it. I knew no churlish proprieties, nor bounds, nor divisions:

but all proprieties and divisions were mine: all treasures and the possessors of them. So that with much ado I was corrupted, and made to learn the dirty devices of this world. Which now I unlearn, and become, as it were, a little child again that I may enter into the Kingdom of God.

Thomas Traherne: from *Centuries*

Your enjoyment of the world is never right, till every morning you awake in Heaven; see yourself in your Father's Palace; and look upon the skies, the earth, and the air as Celestial Joys: having such a reverend esteem of all, as if you were among the Angels. The bride of a monarch, in her husband's chamber, hath no such causes of delight as you.

You never enjoy the world aright, till the Sea itself floweth in your veins, till you are clothed with the heavens, and crowned with the stars: and perceive yourself to be the sole heir of the whole world, and more than so, because men are in it who are every one sole heirs as well as you. Till you can sing and rejoice and delight in God, as misers do in gold, and Kings in sceptres, you never enjoy the world.

Till your spirit filleth the whole world, and the stars are your jewels; till you are as familiar with the ways of God in all Ages as with your walk and table: till you are intimately acquainted with that shady nothing out of which the world was made: till you love men so as to desire their happiness, with a thirst equal to the zeal of your own; till you delight in God for being good to all:

you never enjoy the world. Till you more feel it than your private estate, and are more present in the hemisphere, considering the glories and the beauties there, than in your own house: Till you remember how lately you were made, and how wonderful it was when you came into it: and more rejoice in the palace of your glory, than if it had been made but to-day morning.

Yet further, you never enjoy the world aright, till you so love the beauty of enjoying it, that you are covetous and earnest to persuade others to enjoy it. And so perfectly hate the abominable corruption of men in despising it, that you had rather suffer the flames of Hell than willingly be guilty of their error. There is so much blindness and ingratitude and damned folly in it. The world is a mirror of infinite beauty, yet no man sees it. It is a Temple of Majesty, yet no man regards it. It is a region of Light and Peace, did not men disquiet it. It is the Paradise of God. It is more to man since he is fallen than it was before. It is the place of Angels and the Gate of Heaven. When Jacob waked out of his dream, he said *'God is here, and I wist it not. How dreadful is this place! This is none other than the House of God, and the Gate of Heavens.'*

T. Traherne: from *Centuries*

And God shall wipe away all tears from their eyes; and there shall be no more death, neither sorrow nor crying, neither shall there be any more pain: for the former things are passed away.

Revelations 21:4

Sin is behovely but all shall be well and all shall be well
and all manner of thing shall be well.

Juliana of Norwich

All appeared New, and Strange at first, inexpressibly
rare and Delightfull and Beautifull. I was a little Stranger,
which at my Entrance into the World was Saluted and
Surrounded with innumerable Joys. My Knowledge was
Divine, I knew by Intuition those things which, since
my Apostasie, I Collected again by the Highest Reason.
My very Ignorance was advantageous. I seemed as one
Brought into the Estate of Innocence. All Things were
Spotless and Pure and Glorious: yea, and infinitely mine,
and Joyfull and Precious. I knew not that there were any
Sins, or Complaints or Laws. I Dreamed not of Poverties,
Contentions or Vices. All Tears and Quarrels were
hidden from mine Eyes. Everything was at Rest, free and
Immortal. I knew nothing of Sickness or Death or Rents
or Exaction, either for Tribute or Bread. In the Absence
of these I was entertained like an Angel with the Works
of GOD in their Splendour and Glory, I saw all in the
Peace of Eden; Heaven and Earth did Sing my Creator's
Praises, and could not make more Melody to Adam,
than to me. All Time was Eternity, and a Perpetual
Sabbath. Is it not Strange, that an Infant should be Heir
of the whole World, and see those Mysteries which the
Books of the Learned never unfold?

T. Traherne: from *Centuries*

'Still let my tyrants know, I am not doomed to wear
Year after year in gloom, and desolate despair;
A messenger of Hope comes every night to me,
And offers for short life, eternal liberty.

'He comes with western winds, with evening's
    wandering airs,
With that clear dusk of heaven that brings the thickest
    stars,
Winds take a pensive tone, and stars a tender fire,
And visions rise, and change, that kill me with desire.

'Desire for nothing known in my mature years,
When Joy grew mad with awe, at counting future tears.
When, if my spirit's sky was full of flashes warm,
I knew not whence they came, from sun or thunder-
    storm.

'But, first, a hush of peace—a soundless calm descends;
The struggle of distress, and fierce impatience ends;
Mute music soothes my breast – unuttered harmony,
That I could never dream, till Earth was lost to me.

'Then dawns the Invisible; the Unseen its truth reveals;
My outward sense is gone, my inward essence feels:
Its wings are almost free – its home, its harbour found,
Measuring the gulf, it stoops and dares the final bound.

'O! dreadful is the check – intense the agony –
When the ear begins to hear, and the eye begins to see;
When the pulse begins to throb, the brain to think
    again;
The soul to feel the flesh, and the flesh to feel the chain.

'Yet I would lose no sting, would wish no torture less;
The more that anguish racks, the earlier it will bless;
And robed in fires of hell, or bright with heavenly
    shine,
If it but herald death, the vision is divine!'

Emily Brontë

Last Lines

'The following are the last lines my sister Emily ever wrote.'
(Charlotte Brontë)

No coward soul is mine,
No trembler in the world's storm-troubled sphere:
I see heaven's glories shine,
And faith shines equal, arming me from fear.

O God within my breast,
Almighty, ever-present Deity!
Life – that in me has rest,
As I – undying Life – have power in thee!

Vain are the thousand creeds
That move men's hearts: unutterably vain;
Worthless as withered weeds,
Or idlest froth amid the boundless main,

To waken doubt in one
Holding so fast by thine infinity;
So surely anchored on
The steadfast rock of immortality.

With wide-embracing love
Thy spirit animates eternal years,
Pervades and broods above,
Changes, sustains, dissolves, creates, and rears.

Though earth and man were gone,
And suns and universes ceased to be,
And thou were left alone,
Every existence would exist in thee.

There is not room for Death,
Nor atom that his might could render void:
Thou – thou art Being and Breath,
And what thou art may never be destroyed.

Emily Brontë

Uphill

Does the road wind uphill all the way?
    Yes, to the very end.
Will the day's journey take the whole long day?
    From morn to night, my friend.

But is there for the night a resting-place?
    A roof for when the slow, dark hours begin.
May not the darkness hide it from my face?
    You cannot miss that inn.

Shall I meet other wayfarers at night?
    Those who have gone before.
Then must I knock, or call when just in sight?
    They will not keep you standing at that door.

Shall I find comfort, travel-sore and weak?
    Of labour you shall find the sum.
Will there be beds for me and all who seek?
    Yea, beds for all who come.

                            Christina Rosetti

They are all gone into the world of light!
    And I alone sit lingering here;
Their very memory is fair and bright,
    And my sad thoughts doth clear.

It glows and glitters in my cloudy breast
    Like stars upon some gloomy grove,
Or those faint beams in which this hill is dressed,
    After the sun's remove.

I see them walking in an air of glory,
    Whose light doth trample on my days:
My days, which were at best but dull and hoary,
    Mere glimmering and decays.

O holy Hope! and high Humility,
    High as the heavens above!
These are your walks, and you have showed them me,
    To kindle my cold love.

Dear beauteous Death! the jewel of the Just,
 Shining nowhere but in the dark;
What mysteries do lie beyond thy dust,
 Could man outlook that mark!

He that hath found some fledged bird's nest may know,
 At first sight, if the bird be flown;
But what fair well or grove he sings in now,
 That is to him unknown.

And yet, as angels in some brighter dreams
 Call to the soul, when man doth sleep;
So some strange thoughts transcend our wonted themes,
 And into glory peep.

If a star were confined into a tomb,
 Her captive flames must needs burn there;
But when the hand that locked her up gives room,
 She'll shine through all the sphere.

O Father of eternal life, and all
 Created glories under thee!
Resume thy spirit from this world of thrall
 Into true liberty.

Either disperse these mists, which blot and fill
 My perspective still as they pass,
Or else remove me hence unto that hill,
 Where I shall need no glass.

        Henry Vaughan

Out from the hedge, not five yards distant, pours a rush of deep luscious notes, succeeded by the sweetest trills heard by man. It is the nightingale, which tradition assigns to the night only, but which in fact sings as loudly, and to my ear more joyously, in the full sunlight, especially in the morning, and always close to the nest. The sun has moved onward upon his journey, and this spot is no longer completely shaded, but the foliage of a great oak breaks the force of his rays, and the eye can even bear to gaze at his disc for a few moments. Living for this brief hour at least in unalloyed sympathy with nature, apart from all disturbing influences, the sight of that splendid disc carries the soul with it till it feels as eternal as the sun. Let the memory call up a picture of the desert sands of Egypt – upon the kings with the double crown, upon Rameses, upon Sesostris, upon Assurbanipal the burning beams of this very sun descended, filling their veins with tumultous life, three thousand years ago. Lifted up in absorbing thought, the mind feels that these three thousand years are in truth no longer past than the last beat of the pulse. It throbbed – the throb is gone; their pulse throbbed, and it seems but a moment since, for to thought, as to the sun, there is no time. This little petty life of seventy years, with its little petty aims and hopes, its despicable fears and contemptible sorrows, is no more the life with which the mind is occupied. This golden disc has risen and set, as the graven marks of man alone record, full eight thousand years. The hieroglyphs of the rocks speak of a fiery sun shining inconceivable ages before that. Yet even this almost immortal sun had a beginning – perhaps emerging as a ball of incandescent gas from chaos: how long ago was that? And onwards, still onwards goes the disc, doubtless for ages and ages to come. It is time that our measures should be extended; these paltry divisions of hours and

days and years – aye, of centuries – should be superseded
by terms conveying some faint idea at least of the vastness
of space. For in truth, when thinking thus there is no
time at all. The mind loses the sense of time and reposes
in eternity. This hour, this instant, is eternity; it extends
backwards, it extends forwards, and we are in it. It is a
grand and an ennobling feeling to know that at this
moment illimitable time extends on either hand. No
conception formed in the brain has ever or will ever
surpass the mystery of this endless existence as exemplified
– as made manifest by the physical sun – a visible sign of
immortality. This – this hour is part of the immortal life.
Reclining upon this rug under the chestnut tree, while
the grateful shadows dance, a passing bee hums and the
nightingale sings, while the oak foliage sprinkles the
sunshine over us, we are really and in truth in the midst
of eternity. Only by walking hand in hand with nature,
only by a reverent and loving study of the mysteries for
ever around us, is it possible to disabuse the mind of the
narrow view, the contracted belief that time is now and
eternity to-morrow. Eternity is to-day. The goldfinches
and the tiny caterpillars, the brilliant sun, if looked at
lovingly and thoughtfully, will lift the soul out of the
smaller life of human care that is of selfish aims, bounded
by seventy years, into the greater, the limitless life which
has been going on over universal space from endless ages
past, which is going on now, and which will for ever
and for ever, in one form, or another, continue to
proceed.

Richard Jefferies: from *Nature and Eternity*

Sweetly the summer air came up to the tumulus, the grass sighed softly, the butterflies went by, sometimes alighting on the green dome. Two thousand years! Summer after summer the blue butterflies had visited the mound, the thyme had flowered, the wind sighed in the grass. The azure morning had spread its arms over the low tomb; and full glowing noon burned on it; the purple of sunset rosied the sward. Stars, ruddy in the vapour of the southern horizon, beamed at midnight through the mystic summer night, which is dusky and yet full of light. White mists swept up and hid it; dews rested on the turf; tender harebells drooped; the wings of the finches fanned the air – finches whose colours faded from the wings how many centuries ago! Brown autumn dwelt in the woods beneath; the rime of winter whitened the beech clump on the ridge; again the buds came on the wind-blown hawthorn bushes, and in the evening the broad constellation of Orion covered the east. Two thousand times! Two thousand times the woods grew green, and ring-doves built their nests. Day and night for two thousand years – light and shadow sweeping over the mound – two thousand years of labour by day and slumber by night. Mystery gleaming in the stars, pouring down in the sunshine, speaking in the night, the wonder of the sun and of far space, for twenty centuries round about this low and green-grown dome. Yet all that mystery and wonder is as nothing to the Thought that lies therein, to the spirit that I feel so close.

Realising that spirit, recognising my own inner consciousness, the psyche, so clearly, I cannot understand time. It is eternity now. I am in the midst of it. It is about me in the sunshine; I am in it, as the butterfly floats in the light-laden air. Nothing has to come; it is now. Now is eternity; now is the immortal life. Here this moment, by this tumulus, on earth, now; I exist in it. The years, the centuries, the cycles are absolutely nothing; it is only a moment since this tumulus was raised; in a thousand years more it will still be only a moment. To the soul there is no past and no future; all is and will be ever, in now. For artificial purposes time is mutually agreed on, but there is really no such thing. The shadow goes on upon the dial, the index moves round upon the clock, and what is the difference? None whatever. If the clock had never been set going, what would have been the difference? There may be time for the clock, the clock may make time for itself; there is none for me.

I dip my hand in the brook and feel the stream; in an instant the particles of water which first touched me have floated yards down the current, my hand remains there. I take my hand away, and the flow – the time – of the brook does not exist to me. The great clock of the firmament, the sun and the stars, the crescent moon, the earth circling two thousand times, is no more to me than the flow of the brook when my hand is withdrawn; my soul has never been, and never can be, dipped in time. Time has never existed, and never will; it is a purely artificial arrangement. It is eternity now, it always was eternity, and always will be. By no possible means could I get into time if I tried. I am in eternity now and must there remain. Haste not, be at rest, this Now is eternity. Because the idea of time has left my mind – if ever it had any hold on it – to me the man interred in the tumulus is living, now as I live. We are both in eternity.

Richard Jefferies: from *The Story of My Heart*

Peace

My soul, there is a country
   far beyond the stars,
Where stands a wingèd sentry
   All skilful in the wars:
There above noise and danger
   Sweet Peace sits crowned with smiles,
And One born in a manger
   Commands the beauteous files.
He is thy gracious friend
   And – O my soul, awake! –
Did in pure love descend
   To die here for thy sake.
If thou canst get but thither,
   There grows the flower of Peace,
The Rose that cannot wither,
   Thy fortress, and thy ease.
Leave then thy foolish ranges
   For none can thee secure,
But one who never changes,
   Thy God, thy life, thy cure.

Henry Vaughan

Eternity

He who bends to himself a joy
Does the wingèd life destroy;
But he who kisses the joy as it flies
Lives in eternity's sunrise.

William Blake

O how I long to travel back
And tread again that ancient track!
That I might once more reach that plain
Where first I left my glorious train,
From whence th'Enlightened spirit sees
That shady city of palm-trees;
But (ah!) my soul with too much stay
Is drunk, and staggers in the way.
Some men a forward motion love,
But I by backward steps would move,
And when this dust falls to the urn,
In that state I came, return.

Henry Vaughan

9

Agnostics, Atheists, Humanists and Rationalists

Secular Attitudes to Death

Here we stand before the abyss. It is void of all the dreams with which our fathers peopled it. They thought that they knew what was there; we know only what is not there. It has enlarged itself with all that we have learnt to know nothing of. While waiting for a scientific certainty to break through its darkness – for man has the right to hope for that which he does not yet conceive – the only point that interests us, because it is situated in the little circle which our actual intelligence traces in the thickest blackness of the night, is to know whether the unknown for which we are bound will be dreadful or not.

Outside the religions, there are four imaginable solutions and no more: total annihilation; survival with our consciousness of to-day; survival without any sort of consciousness; lastly, survival with universal consciousness different from that which we possess in this world.

Total annihilation is impossible. We are the prisoners of an infinity without outlet, wherein nothing perishes, wherein everything is dispersed, but nothing lost. Neither a body nor a thought can drop out of the universe, out of time and space. Not an atom of our flesh, not a quiver

of our nerves, will go where they will cease to be, for
there is no place where anything ceases to be. The
brightness of a star extinguished millions of years ago
still wanders in the ether where our eyes will perhaps
behold it this very night, pursuing its endless road. It is
the same with all that we see, as with all that we do not
see. To be able to do away with a thing, that is to say, to
fling it into nothingness, nothingness would have to
exist; and, if it exist, under whatever form, it is no longer
nothingness. As soon as we try to analyze it, to define it,
or to understand it, thoughts and expressions fail us, or
create that which they are struggling to deny. It is as
contrary to the nature of our reason and probably of all
imaginable reason to conceive nothingness as to conceive
limits to infinity.

Maurice Maeterlinck: from *Death*

An Arundel Tomb

Side by side, their faces blurred,
The earl and countess lie in stone,
Their proper habits vaguely shown
As jointed armour, stiffened pleat,
And that faint hint of the absurd –
The little dogs under their feet.

Such plainness of the pre-baroque
Hardly involves the eye, until
It meets his left-hand gauntlet, still
Clasped empty in the other; and
One sees, with a sharp tender shock,
His hand withdrawn, holding her hand.

They would not think to lie so long.
Such faithfulness in effigy
Was just a detail friends would see:
A sculptor's sweet commissioned grace
Thrown off in helping to prolong
The Latin names around the base.

They would not guess how early in
Their supine stationary voyage
The air would change to soundless damage,
Turn the old tenantry away;
How soon succeeding eyes begin
To look, not read. Rigidly they

Persisted, linked, through lengths and breadths
Of time. Snow fell, undated. Light
Each summer thronged the glass. A bright
Litter of birdcalls strewed the same
Bone-riddled ground. And up the paths
The endless altered people came,

Washing at their identity.
Now, helpless in the hollow of
An unarmorial age, a trough
Of smoke in slow suspended skeins
Above their scrap of history,
Only an attitude remains:

Time has transfigured them into
Untruth. The stone fidelity
They hardly meant has come to be
Their final blazon, and to prove
Our almost-instinct almost true:
What will survive of us is love.

Philip Larkin

The Great Minimum

It is something to have wept as we have wept,
It is something to have done as we have done,
It is something to have watched when all men slept,
And seen the stars which never see the sun. . . .

. . . Lo, blessed are our ears for they have heard;
Yea, blessed are our eyes for they have seen;
Let thunder break on man and beast and bird
And the lightning. It is something to have been.

G. K. Chesterton

And call to recollection both how many things thou hast
passed through, and how many things thou hast been
able to endure and that the history of thy life is now
complete and thy service is ended; and how many
beautiful things thou hast seen; and how many pleasures
and pains thou hast despised; and how many things
called honourable thou hast spurned; and to how many
ill-minded folks thou hast shown a kind disposition.

Marcus Aurelius
translated by George Long

Mortal man, you have been a citizen in this great City; what does it matter to you whether for five or fifty years? For what is according to its law is equal for every man. Why is it hard, then, if Nature who brought you in, and no despot nor unjust judge, sends you out of the City – as though the master of the show, who engaged an actor, were to dismiss him from the stage? 'But I have not spoken my five acts, only three.' 'What you say is true, but in life three acts are the whole play.' For He determines the perfect whole, the cause yesterday of your composition, today of your dissolution; you are the cause of neither. Leave the stage, therefore, and be reconciled, for He also who lets his servant depart is reconciled.

Marcus Aurelius: *Meditations*,
translated by George Long

Laodameia died; Helen died; Leda, the beloved of Jupiter, went before. It is better to repose in the earth betimes than to sit up late; better than to cling pertinaciously to what we feel crumbling under us, and to protract an inevitable fall. We may enjoy the present while we are insensible of infirmity and decay: but the present, like a note in music, is nothing but as it appertains to what is past and what is to come. There are no fields of amaranth on this side of the grave: there are no voices, O Rhodope, that are not soon mute, however tuneful: there is no name, with whatever emphasis of passionate love repeated, of which the echo is not faint at last.

Walter Savage Landor

But for your Terror
Where would be Valour?
What is Love for
   But to stand in your way?
Taker and Giver,
For all your endeavour
You leave us with more
   Than you touch with decay.

                              Oliver St. John Gogarty

My candle burns at both ends;
   It will not last the night;
But, ah, my foes, and oh, my friends,
   It gives a lovely light!

                              Edna St. Vincent Millay

There were grass-grown tumuli on the hills to which of old I used to walk, sit down at the foot of one of them, and think. Some warrior had been interred there in the ante-historic times. The sun of the summer morning shone on the dome of sward, and the air came softly up from the wheat below, the tips of the grasses swayed as it passed sighing faintly, it ceased, and the bees hummed by to the thyme and heathbells. I became absorbed in the glory of the day, the sunshine, the sweet air, the yellowing corn turning from its sappy green to summer's noon of gold, the lark's song like a waterfall in the sky. I felt at that moment that I was like the spirit of the man whose body was interred in the tumulus; I could understand and feel his existence the same as my own. He was as real to me two thousand years after interment as those I had seen in the body. The abstract personality of the dead seemed as existent as thought. As my thought could slip back the twenty centuries in a moment to the forest-days when he hurled the spear, or shot with the bow, hunting the deer, and could return again as swiftly to this moment, so his spirit could endure from then till now, and the time was nothing.

Two thousand years being a second to the soul could not cause its extinction. It was no longer to the soul than my thought occupied to me. Recognising my own inner consciousness, the psyche, so clearly, death did not seem to me to affect the personality. In dissolution there was no bridgeless chasm, no unfathomable gulf of separation; the spirit did not immediately become inaccessible, leaping at a bound to an immeasurable distance. Look at another person while living; the soul is not visible, only the body which it animates. Therefore, merely because after death the soul is not visible is no demonstration that it does not still live. The condition of being unseen is the same condition which occurs while the body is living, so that intrinsically there is nothing exceptional, or supernatural, in the life of the soul after death. Resting by the tumulus, the spirit of the man who had been interred there was to me really alive, and very close. This was quite natural, as natural and simple as the grass waving in the wind, the bees humming, and the larks' songs. Only by the strongest effort of the mind could I understand the idea of extinction; that was supernatural, requiring a miracle; the immortality of the soul natural, like earth. Listening to the sighing of the grass I felt immortality as I felt the beauty of the summer morning, and I thought beyond immortality, of other conditions, more beautiful than existence, higher than immortality.

That there is no knowing, in the sense of written reasons, whether the soul lives on or not, I am fully aware. I do not hope or fear. At least while I am living I have enjoyed the idea of immortality, and the idea of my own soul. If then, after death, I am resolved without exception into earth, air, and water, and the spirit goes out like a flame, still I shall have had the glory of that thought.

Richard Jefferies: from *The Story of my Heart*

There is no separation – no past; eternity, the Now, is continuous. When all the stars have revolved they only produce Now again. The continuity of Now is for ever. So that it appears to me purely natural, and not supernatural, that the soul whose temporary frame was interred in this mound should be existing as I sit on the sward. How infinitely deeper is thought than the million miles of the firmament! The wonder is here, not there; now, not to be, now always. Things that have been miscalled supernatural appear to me simple, more natural than nature, than earth, than sea, or sun. It is beyond telling more natural that I should have a soul than not, that there should be immortality; I think there is much more than immortality. It is matter which is the supernatural, and difficult of understanding. Why this clod of earth I hold in my hand? Why this water which drops sparkling from my fingers dipped in the brook? Why are they at all? When? How? What for? Matter is beyond understanding, mysterious, impenetrable; I touch it easily, comprehend it, no. Soul, mind – the thought, the idea – is easily understood, it understands itself and is conscious.

The supernatural miscalled, the natural in truth, is the real. To me everything is supernatural. How strange that condition of mind which cannot accept anything but the earth, the sea, the tangible universe! Without the misnamed supernatural these to me seem incomplete, unfinished. Without soul all these are dead. Except when I walk by the sea, and my soul is by it, the sea is dead. Those seas by which no man has stood – by which no soul has been – whether on earth or the planets, are dead. No matter how majestic the planet rolls in space, unless a soul be there it is dead. As I move about in the sunshine I feel in the midst of the supernatural: in the midst of immortal things. It is impossible to wrest the mind down to the same laws that rule pieces of timber, water, or earth. They do not control the soul, however rigidly they may bind matter. So full am I always of a sense of the immortality now at this moment round about me, that it would not surprise me in the least if a circumstance

outside physical experience occurred. It would seem to
me quite natural. Give the soul the power it conceives,
and there would be nothing wonderful in it.

Richard Jefferies: from *The Story of My Heart*

Vanitas Vanitatum

All the flowers of the spring
Meet to perfume our burying;
These have but their growing prime,
And man does flourish but his time:
Survey our progress from our birth –
We are set, we grow, we turn to earth.
Courts adieu, and all delights,
All bewitching appetites!
Sweetest breath and clearest eye
Like perfumes go out and die;
And consequently this is done
As shadows wait upon the sun.
Vain the ambition of kings
Who seek by trophies and dead things
To leave a living name behind,
And weave but nets to catch the wind.

John Webster

To Daffodils

Fair daffodils, we weep to see
    You haste away so soon;
As yet the early-rising sun
    Hast not attained his noon.
        Stay, stay
        Until the hasting day
        Has run
        But to the evensong;
And, having prayed together, we
    Will go with you along.

We have short time to stay as you,
    We have as short a spring;
As quick a growth to meet decay,
    As you, or anything.
        We die
        As your hours do, and dry
        Away
        Like to the summer's rain;
Or as the pearls of morning's dew,
    Ne'er to be found again.

Robert Herrick

All That's Past

Very old are the woods;
　　And the buds that break
Out of the brier's boughs,
　　When March winds wake,
So old with their beauty are –
　　Oh, no man knows
Through what wild centuries
　　Roves back the rose.

Very old are the brooks;
　　And the rills that rise
Where snow sleeps cold beneath
　　The azure skies
Sing such a history
　　Of come and gone,
Their every drop is as wise
　　As Solomon.

Very old are we men;
　　Our dreams are tales
Told in dim Eden
　　By Eve's nightingales;
We wake and whisper awhile,
　　But, the day gone by,
Silence and sleep like fields
　　Of amaranth lie.

                                              Walter De la Mare

Transformations

Portion of this yew
Is a man my grandsire knew,
Bosomed here at its foot:
This branch may be his wife,
A ruddy human life
Now turned to a green shoot.

These grasses must be made
Of her who often prayed,
Last century, for repose;
And the fair girl long ago
Whom I often tried to know
May be entering this rose.

So, they are not underground,
But as nerves and veins abound
In the growths of upper air,
And they feel the sun and rain,
And the energy again
That made them what they were!

Thomas Hardy

Death devours all lovely things;
     Lesbia with her sparrow
Shares the darkness – presently
     Every bed is narrow.

Edna St. Vincent Millay

Man is only a reed, the weakest thing in nature – but a thinking reed. It does not take the universe in arms to crush him; a vapour, a drop of water, is enough to kill him. But, though the universe should crush him, man would still be nobler than his destroyer, because he knows that he is dying, that the universe has the advantage of him; the universe knows nothing of this.

Blaise Pascal: Penseés (translated D. J. Enright)

If I should go before the rest of you
Break not a flower nor inscribe a stone,
Nor when I'm gone speak in a Sunday voice
But be the usual selves that I have known.
    Weep if you must,
    Parting is hell,
    But life goes on,
    So sing as well.

Joyce Grenfell

Do not despise death, but be well content with it, since this too is one of those things which nature wills. For such as it is to be young and to grow old, and to increase and to reach maturity, and to have teeth and beard and gray hairs, and to beget and to be pregnant and to bring forth, and all the other natural operations which the seasons of thy life bring, such also is dissolution. This, then, is consistent with the character of a reflecting man, – to be neither careless nor impatient nor contemptuous with respect to death but to wait for it as one of the operations of nature.

Marcus Aurelius

My prime of youth is but a frost of cares;
   My feast of joy is but a dish of pain;
My crop of corn is but a field of tares;
   And all my good is but vain hope of gain:
The day is past, and yet I saw no sun;
And now I live, and now my life is done.

My tale was heard, and yet it was not told;
   My fruit is fall'n, and yet my leaves are green;
My youth is spent, and yet I am not old;
   I saw the world, and yet I was not seen;
My thread is cut, and yet it is not spun;
And now I live, and now my life is done.

I sought my death, and found it in my womb;
   I looked for life, and saw it was a shade;
I trod the earth, and knew it was my tomb;
   And now I die, and now I was but made:
My glass is full, and now my glass is run;
And now I live, and now my life is done.

Chidiock Tichborne:
Elegy, written in the Tower before his execution

The Sick Soul

To ascribe religious value to mere happy-go-lucky contentment with one's brief chance at natural good is but the very consecration of forgetfulness and superficiality. Our troubles lie indeed too deep for *that* cure. The fact that we *can* die, that we *can* be ill at all, is what perplexes us; the fact that we now for a moment live and are well is irrelevant to that perplexity. We need a life not correlated with death, a health not liable to illness, a kind of good that will not perish, a good in fact that flies beyond the Goods of nature.

It all depends on how sensitive the soul may become to discords. 'The trouble with me is that I believe too much in common happiness and goodness,' said a friend of mine whose consciousness was of this sort, 'and nothing can console me for their transiency. I am appalled and disconcerted at its being possible.' And so with most of us: a little cooling down of animal excitability and instinct, a little loss of animal toughness, a little irritable weakness and descent of the pain-threshold, will bring the worm at the core of all our usual springs of delight into full view, and turn us into melancholy metaphysicians. The pride of life and glory of the world will shrivel. It is after all but the standing quarrel of hot youth and hoary old. Old age has the last word: the purely naturalistic look at life, however enthusiastically it may begin, is sure to end in sadness.

This sadness lies at the heart of every merely positivistic, agnostic, or naturalistic scheme of philosophy.

*   *   *

The lustre of the present hour is always borrowed from the background of possibilities it goes with. Let our common experiences be enveloped in an eternal moral order; let our suffering have an immortal significance; let Heaven smile upon the earth, and deities pay their visits; let faith and hope be the atmosphere which man breathes in; – and his days pass by with zest; they stir with prospects, they thrill with remoter values. Place round them on the contrary the curdling cold and gloom and absence of all permanent meaning which for pure naturalism and the popular science evolutionism of our time are all that is visible ultimately, and the thrill stops short, or turns rather to an anxious trembling.

William James: from *The Varieties of Religious Experience*

In these remarks I am leaning only upon mankind's common instinct for reality, which in point of fact has always held the world to be essentially a theatre for heroism. In heroism, we feel, life's supreme mystery is hidden. We tolerate no one who has no capacity whatever for it in any direction. On the other hand, no matter what a man's frailties otherwise may be, if he be willing to risk death, and still more if he suffer it heroically, in the service he has chosen, the fact consecrates him forever. Inferior to ourselves in this or that way, if yet we cling to life, and he is able 'to fling it away like a flower' as caring nothing for it, we account him in the deepest way our born superior. Each of us in his own person feels that a high-hearted indifference to life would expiate all his shortcomings.

The metaphysical mystery, thus recognized by common sense, that he who feeds on death that feeds on men possesses life supereminently and excellently, and meets best the secret demands of the universe, is the truth of which asceticism has been the faithful champion. The folly of the cross, so inexplicable by the intellect, has yet its indestructible vital meaning.

Representatively, then, and symbolically, and apart from the vagaries into which the unenlightened intellect of former times may have let it wander, asceticism must, I believe, be acknowledged to go with the profounder way of handling the gift of existence. Naturalistic optimism is mere syllabub and flattery and sponge-cake in comparison.

William James: from *The Varieties of Religious Experience*

The love of life, and the fear of death, are distinct things, though they often act reciprocally or conjunctly. It cannot strictly be said that life is valued, because the act or the consequences of quitting it are dreaded. Life may be clung to and fostered on that account, but only for the sake of procrastinating an evil. But, on the other hand, where life is loved, the privation of it must necessarily be an object of fear. If Doctor Johnson's statement of his own feelings may be relied on, he never regarded life otherwise than as a series of suffering; yet no man ever seems to have viewed death with more horror. His gloomy imagination probably conjured up terrific visions of future existence, which his principles were unable to dispel . . .

The value of life is the value of all we possess in life. Since, therefore, men universally show a solicitude, greater or less, for the preservation of life, it may be concluded that they universally feel they have something valuable to lose, either in possession or in expectation. But, as before observed, this attachment to life is in no assignable proportion to external circumstances. It is sometimes weak in the young, the wealthy, the vigorous, with numerous sources of enjoyment courting their acceptance; while it is strong in the indigent, old and valetudinary, to whom existence might be thought a burthen.

The fact is that here as in so many other instances, mind is the true measure of man, and it creates to itself its habitual sentiments and affections, with little dependence on the world without. It may, I think, in general be observed, that the greatest lovers of life are persons of a sanguine temperament, engaged in active pursuits, full of projects for futurity, readily attaching themselves to new objects and new acquaintances, and able to convert every occurrence of life into a matter of importance; – on the other hand the phlegmatic, inactive, dubious, desponding, and indifferent, as soon as the warmth and curiosity of youth are over, frequently become careless about the remainder of life, and rather consent to live on through habit, than feel themselves much interested in the continuance of their existence. . . .

Innocence and contentment – active pursuits during the season of activity, and philosophical contemplation when that is past – will render life a valuable blessing, till disease or decrepitude loosens the bonds of our attachment to it, and nature grants the dismission she has finally provided for all created beings.

John Aiken: from 'Letters from a father to his son',
On the Value of Life

Pierre interrupted him. 'Do you believe in a future life?'
he asked.

'In a future life?' repeated Prince Andrey.

But Pierre did not give him time to answer, and took
this repetition as a negative reply, the more readily as he
knew Prince Andrey's atheistic views in the past. 'You
say that you can't see the dominion of good and truth on
the earth. I have not seen it either, and it cannot be seen
if one looks upon our life as the end of everything. On
earth, this earth here' (Pierre pointed to the open
country), 'there is no truth – all is deception and
wickedness. But in the world, the whole world, there is
a dominion of truth, and we are now the children of
earth, but eternally the children of the whole universe.
Don't I feel in my soul that I am a part of that vast,
harmonious whole? Don't I feel that in that vast,
innumerable multitude of beings, in which is made
manifest the Godhead, the higher power – what you
choose to call it – I constitute one grain, one step upward
from lower beings to higher ones? If I see, see clearly
that ladder that rises up from the vegetable to man, why
should I suppose that ladder breaks off with me and does
not go on further and further? I feel that I cannot
disappear as nothing does disappear in the universe, that
indeed I always shall be and always have been. I feel that
beside me, above me, there are spirits, and that in their
world there is truth'.

Tolstoy: from *War and Peace*
(translated by Constance Garnett)

It would be truly agreeable for any man to sit in well-watered gardens with Mohammed, clad in green silks, drinking delicious sherbets, and transfixed by the gazelle-like glance of some young girl, all innocence and fire. Amid such scenes a man might remain himself and might fulfil hopes that he had actually cherished on earth. He might also find his friends again, which in somewhat generous minds is perhaps the thought that chiefly sustains interest in a posthumous existence. But to recognize his friends a man must find them in their bodies, with their familiar habits, voices, and interests; for it is surely an insult to affection to say that he could find them in an eternal formula expressing their idiosyncrasy. When, however, it is clearly seen that another life, to supplement this one, must closely resemble it, does not the magic of immortality altogether vanish? Is such a reduplication of earthly society at all credible? And the prospect of awakening again among houses and trees, among children and dotards, among wars and rumours of wars, still fettered to one personality and one accidental past, still uncertain of the future, is not this prospect wearisome and deeply repulsive? Having passed through these things once and bequeathed them to posterity, is it not time for each soul to rest?

George Santayana: from *The Life of Reason*

Away, Melancholy

Away, melancholy,
Away with it, let it go.

Are not the trees green,
The earth as green?
Does not the wind blow,
Fire leap and the rivers flow?
Away melancholy.

The ant is busy
He carrieth his meat,
All things hurry
To be eaten or eat.
Away, melancholy.
Man, too, hurries,
Eats, couples, buries,
He is an animal also
With a hey ho melancholy,
Away with it, let it go.

Man of all creatures
Is superlative
(Away melancholy)
He of all creatures alone
Raiseth a stone
(Away melancholy)
Into the stone, the god
Pours what he knows of good
Calling good, God.
Away melancholy, let it go.

Speak not to me of tears,
Tyranny, pox, wars,
Saying, Can God
Stone of man's thought, be good?
Say rather it is enough
That the stuffed
Stone of man's good, growing,
By man's called God.
Away, melancholy, let it go.

Man aspires
To good,
To love
Sighs;

Beaten, corrupted, dying
In his own blood lying
Yet heaves up an eye above
Cries, Love, love.
It is his virtue needs explaining,
Not his failing.

Away, melancholy,
Away with it, let it go.

Stevie Smith

Suppose, then, that after the greatest, most passionate
vividness and tender glory, oblivion is all we have to
expect, the big blank of death. What options present
themselves? One option is to train yourself gradually

into oblivion so that no great change has taken place when you have died. Another option is to increase the bitterness of life so that death is a desirable release. (In this the rest of mankind will fully collaborate.) There is a further option seldom chosen. That option is to let the deepest elements in you disclose their deepest information. If there is nothing but nonbeing and oblivion waiting for us, the prevailing beliefs have not misled us, and that's that. This would astonish me, for the prevailing beliefs seldom satisfy my need for truth. Still the possibility must be allowed.

Saul Bellow: from *Humboldt's Gift*

A Woman's Death

'And she was as white as marble-stone,' said Mrs Cuxsom. 'And likewise such a thoughtful woman, too – ah, poor soul – that a' minded every little thing that wanted tending. "Yes," says she, "when I'm gone, and my last breath's blowed, look in the top drawer o' the chest in the back room by the window, and you'll find all my coffin clothes; a piece of flannel – that's to put under me, and the little piece is to put under my head; and my new stockings for my feet – they are folded alongside, and all my other things. And there's four ounce pennies, the heaviest I could find, a-tied up in bits of linen, for weights – two for my right eye and two for my left," she said. "And when you've used 'em, and my eyes don't open no more, bury the pennies, good souls, and don't ye go spending 'em, for I shouldn't like it. And open the windows as soon as I am carried out, and make it as cheerful as you can for Elizabeth-Jane."'

'Ah, poor heart!' . . .

. . . 'Well, poor soul; she's helpless to hinder that or anything now,' answered Mother Cuxsom. 'And all her shining keys will be took from her, and her cupboards opened; and little things a' didn't wish seen anybody will see; and her wishes and ways will all be as nothing!'

Thomas Hardy: *The Mayor of Casterbridge*

A Good Man Remembered

She stooped down and cleared away the withered flowers that Grace and herself had laid there the previous week, and put her fresh ones in their place.

'Now, my own, own love,' she whispered, 'your are mine, and only mine; for she has forgot 'ee at last, although for her you died! But I – whenever I get up I'll think of 'ee, and whenever I lie down I'll think of 'ee again. Whenever I plant the young larches I'll think that none can plant as you planted; and whenever I split a gad, and whenever I turn the cider wring, I'll say none could do it like you. If ever I forget your name let me forget home and heaven! . . . But no, no, my love, I never can forget 'ee; for you was a good man, and did good things!'

Thomas Hardy: *The Woodlanders*

Sonnet

Not on sad Stygian shore, nor in clear sheen
Of far Elysian plain, shall we meet those
Among the dead whose pupils we have been,
Nor those great shades whom we have felt as foes;
No meadow of asphodel our feet shall tread,
Nor shall we look each other in the face
To love or hate each other being dead,
Hoping some praise or fearing some disgrace.
We shall not argue saying 'Twas thus' or 'Thus',
Our argument's whole drift we shall forget;
Who's right, who's wrong, 'Twill all be one to us;
We shall not even know that we have met.
    Yet meet we shall, and part, and meet again
    Where dead men meet, on lips of living men.

Samuel Butler

If it be a short and violent death, we have no leisure to
fear it; if otherwise, I perceive that according as I engage
myself in sickness, I do naturally fall into some disdain
and contempt of life.

It is uncertain where death looks for us; let us expect
her everywhere: the premeditation of death, is a
forethinking of liberty. He who hath learned to die, hath
unlearned to serve. There is no evil in life, for him that
hath well conceived, how the privation of life is no evil.
To know how to die, doth free us from all subjection
and constraint.

Michel de Montaigne

A free man thinks of death least of all things; and his
wisdom is a meditation not of death but of life.

Spinoza

Not, how did he die, but how did he live?
Not, what did he gain, but what did he give?
These are the units to measure the worth
Of a man as a man, regardless of birth.
Not what was his church, nor what was his creed?
But had he befriended those really in need?
Was he ever ready, with word of good cheer,
To bring back a smile, to banish a tear?
Not what did the sketch in the newspaper say,
But how many were sorry when he passed away?

Anon

The death of Socrates

What is this strange outcry? he said. I sent away the
women that they might not offend in this way, for I
have heard that a man should die in peace. Be quiet, then,
and have patience!
    When we heard that, we were ashamed, and refrained
our tears; and he walked about until, as he said, his legs
began to fail; and then he lay on his back according to

the directions, and the man who gave him the poison now and then looked at his feet and legs; and after a while he pressed his foot hard and asked him if he could feel, and he said No.

He felt them himself and said: 'When the poison reaches the heart, that will be the end.' He was beginning to grow cold about the groin when he uncovered his face and said (they were his last words): 'Crito, I owe a cock to Asclepius. Will you remember to pay the debt?' 'The debt shall be paid,' said Crito. 'Is there anything else?' There was no answer to this question. But in a minute or two a movement was heard, and the attendants uncovered him. His eyes were set, and Crito closed his eyes and mouth.

Such was the end of our friend, whom I may truly call the wisest, justest, and best of all the men whom I have ever known.

Plato: *Phaedo*

Gently they go, the beautiful, the tender, the kind;
Quietly they go, the intelligent, the witty, the brave.
I know. But I do not approve. And I am not resigned.

Edna St. Vincent Millay

To Travel Hopefully is Better than to Arrive

A strange picture we make on our way to our chimeras, ceaselessly marching, grudging ourselves the time for rest: indefatigable, adventurous pioneers.

It is true that we shall never reach the goal; it is even more than probable that there is no such place; and if we lived for centuries and were endowed with the powers of a god we should find ourselves not much nearer what we wanted at the end. O toiling hands of mortals! O unwearied feet, travelling ye know not whither! Soon, soon it seems to you, you must come forth on some conspicuous hilltop, and but a little way farther, against the setting sun, descry the spires of El Dorado. Little do ye know your own blessedness, for to travel hopefully is a better thing than to arrive, and the true success is to labour.

Robert Louis Stevenson

When

When mine hour is come
Let no teardrop fall
And no darkness hover
Round me where I lie.
Let the vastness call
One who was its lover,
Let me breathe the sky.

> Where the lordly light
> Walks along the world,
> And its silent tread
> Leaves the grasses bright,
> Leaves the flowers uncurled,
> Let me to the dead
> Breathe a gay good-night.

AE. (George Russell)

LIFE IS THE COMPANION OF DEATH, AND DEATH IS THE BEGINNING OF LIFE. Who can appreciate the connection between the two? When a man is born, it is but the embodiment of a spirit. When the spirit is embodied, there is life, and when the spirit disperses, there is death. But if life and death are companions to each other, why should I be concerned? Therefore, all things are one. What we love is the mystery of life. What we hate is corruption in death. But the corruptible in its turn becomes mysterious life, and this mysterious life once more becomes corruptible.

THE AGITATIONS OF MAN'S SOUL. For whether the soul is locked in sleep or whether in waking hours the body moves, we are striving and struggling with the immediate circumstances. Some are easy-going and leisurely, some are deep and cunning, and some are secretive. Now we are frightened over petty fears, now disheartened and dismayed over some great terror. Now the mind flies forth like an arrow from a crossbow, to be the arbiter of right and wrong. Now it stays behind as if sworn to an oath, to hold on to what it has secured.

Then, as under autumn and winter's blight, comes gradual decay, and submerged in its own occupations, it keeps on running its course, never to return. Finally, worn out and imprisoned, it is choked up like an old drain, and the failing mind shall not see light again.

Joy and anger, sorrow and happiness, worries and regrets, hesitation and fears, come upon us by turns, with ever-changing moods, like music from the hollows, or like mushrooms from damp. Day and night they alternate within us, but we cannot tell whence they spring. Alas! Alas! Could we for a moment lay our finger upon their very Cause?

But for these emotions I should not be. Yet but for me, there would be no one to feel them. So far we can go; but we do not know by whose order they come into play. It would seem there was a soul; but the clue to its existence is wanting. That it functions is credible enough, thought we cannot see its form. Perhaps it has inner reality without outward form.

The Wisdom of Laotse, translated Lin Yutang

Silence

There is a silence where hath been no sound,
   There is a silence where no sound may be,
   In the cold grave – under the deep, deep sea,
Or in wide desert where no life is found,
Which hath been mute, and still must sleep profound;
   No voice is hushed – no life treads silently,
   But clouds and cloudy shadows wander free,

That never spoke, over the idle ground:
But in green ruins, in the desolate walls,
    Of antique palaces, where Man hath been,
Though the dun fox, or wild hyena, calls,
    And owls, that flit continually between,
Shriek to the echo, and the low winds moan,
There the true Silence is, self-conscious and alone.

Thomas Hood

Wanderer's Night-Song

Over all the hill tops
Lies peace.
In all the tree tops
You sense
Scarce a breath;
The little birds are silent in the forest.
Wait, only wait, and soon
You too will
Lie in peace.

Goethe (transl. J. Benn)

Life
Animula, vagula, blandula

Life! I know not what thou art,
But know that thou and I must part;
And when, or how, or where we met,
I own to me's a secret yet.
But this I know, when thou art fled,
Where'er they lay these limbs, this head,
No clod so valueless shall be,
As all that then remains of me.
O whither, whither dost thou fly,
Where bend unseen thy trackless course,
    And in this strange divorce,
Ah tell where I must seek this compound I?

To the vast ocean of empyreal flame,
   From whence thy essence came,
   Dost thou thy flight pursue, when freed
   From matter's base encumbering weed?
     Or dost thou, hid from sight,
     Wait, like some spell-bound knight,
Through blank oblivious years the' appointed hour,
To break thy trance and reassume thy power?
Yet canst thou without thought or feeling be?
O say what art thou, when no more thou'rt thee?

 Life! we've been long together,
 Through pleasant and through cloudy weather;
   'Tis hard to part when friends are dear;
   Perhaps 't will cost a sigh, a tear;
   Then steal away, give little warning,
     Choose thine own time;
 Say not Good night, but in some brighter clime
    Bid me Good morning.

Anna Lætitia Barbauld

Who are you?
Do you not know me? Have you not expected me?
Where do you carry me?
Come with me and you shall know.
The way is dark.
Yes; but it is well trodden.

Anna Lætitia Barbauld

Sudden Light

I have been here before,
But when or how I cannot tell:
I know the grass beyond the door,
The sweet keen smell,
The sighing sound, the lights around the shore.

You have been mine before, –
How long ago I may not know:
But just when at that swallow's soar
Your neck turned so,
Some veil did fall, – I knew it all of yore.

Has this been thus before?
And shall not thus time's eddying flight
Still with our lives our love restore
In death's despite,
And day and night yield one delight once more.

Dante Gabriel Rossetti

Here, in this little Bay,
Full of tumultuous life and great repose,
Where, twice a day,
The purposeless, glad ocean comes and goes,
Under high cliffs, and far from the huge town,
I sit me down.
For want of me the world's course will not fail:
When all its work is done, the lie shall rot;
The truth is great, and shall prevail,
When none cares whether it prevail or not.

Coventry Patmore

There is No Death

There is no death! The stars go down
    To rise upon some fairer shore:
And bright in heaven's jewelled crown
    They shine for evermore.

There is no death! The dust we tread
    Shall change beneath the summer showers
To golden grain or mellowed fruit,
    Or rainbow-tinted flowers.

There is no death! The leaves may fall,
    And flowers may fade and pass away;
They only wait, through wintry hours,
    The coming of the May.

And ever near us, though unseen,
   The dear immortal spirits tread;
For all the boundless universe
   Is life – there are no dead.

J. L. McCreery

O may I join the choir invisible
Of those immortal dead who live again
In minds made better by their presence: live
In pulses stirred to generosity,
In deeds of daring rectitude, in scorn
For miserable aims that end with self,
In thoughts sublime that pierce the night like stars,
And with their mild persistence urge man's search
To vaster issues . . .
                This is the life to come,
Which martyred men have made more glorious
For us who strive to follow. May I reach
That purest heaven, be to other souls
The cup of strength in some great agony,
Enkindle generous ardour, feed pure love,
Beget the smiles that have no cruelty –
Be the sweet presence of a good diffused,
And in diffusion ever more intense.
So shall I join the choir invisible
Whose music is the gladness of the world.

George Eliot

Mimnermus in Church

You promise heavens free from strife,
　Pure truth, and perfect change of will;
But sweet, sweet is this human life,
　So sweet, I fain would breathe it still;
Your chilly stars I can forgo,
This warm kind world is all I know.

You say there is no substance here,
　One great reality above:
Back from that void I shrink in fear,
　And child-like hide myself in love:
Show me what angels feel. Till then
I cling, a mere weak man, to men.

You bid me lift my means desires
　From faltering lips and fitful veins
To sexless souls, ideal quires,
　Unwearied voices, wordless strains:
My mind with fonder welcome owns
One dear dead friend's remembered tones.

Forsooth the present we must give
　To that which cannot pass away;
All beauteous things for which we live
　By laws of time and space decay.
But Oh, the very reason why
I clasp them, is because they die.

William Cory

They are not long, the weeping and the laughter,
    Love and desire and hate
I think they have no portion in us after
        We pass the gate.

They are not long, the days of wine and roses:
    Out of a misty dream
Our path emerges for a while, then closes
        Within a dream.

                                        Ernest Dowson

Say Not the Struggle Nought Availeth

Say not the struggle nought availeth,
    The labour and the wounds are vain,
The enemy faints not, nor faileth,
    And as things have been, things remain.

If hopes were dupes, fears may be liars;
    It may be, in yon smoke concealed,
Your comrades chase e'en now the fliers,
    And, but for you, possess the field.

For while the tired waves, vainly breaking,
    Seem here no painful inch to gain,
Far back through creeks and inlets making
    Came, silent, flooding in, the main,

And not by eastern windows only,
    When daylight comes, comes in the light,
In front the sun climbs slow, how slowly,
    But westward, look, the land is bright.

                        Arthur Hugh Clough

Out of the night that covers me,
    Black as the Pit from pole to pole,
I thank whatever gods may be
    For my unconquerable soul.

In the fell clutch of circumstance
    I have not winced nor cried aloud.
Under the bludgeonings of chance
    My head is bloody, but unbowed.

Beyond this place of wrath and tears
    Looms but the Horror of the shade,
And yet the menace of the years
    Finds, and shall find, me unafraid.

It matters not how strait the gate,
    How charged with punishments the scroll,
I am the master of my fate:
    I am the captain of my soul

                        William Ernest Henley

Come, cheerful day, part of my life, to me:
For while thou view'st me with thy fading light,
Part of my life doth still depart with thee,
And I still onward haste to my last night.
   Time's fatal wings do ever forward fly,
   So every day we live a day we die.

But, O ye nights, ordained for barren rest,
How are my days deprived of life in you,
When heavy sleep my soul hath dispossest,
By feignèd death life sweetly to renew!
   Part of my life in that, you life deny:
   So every day we live, a day we die.

Thomas Campion

What if a day, or a month, or a year
Crown thy delights with a thousand sweet contentings?
Cannot a chance of a night or an hour
Cross they desires with as many sad tormentings?
   Fortune, honour, beauty, youth
   Are but blossoms dying;
   Wanton pleasure, doting love,
   Are but shadows flying.
   All our joys are but toys,
   Idle thoughts deceiving;
   None hath power of an hour
   In their lives bereaving.

Earth's but a point to the world, and a man
Is but a point to the world's comparëd centre:
Shall then the point of a point be so vain
As to triumph in a silly point's adventure?
    All is hazard that we have,
    There is nothing biding;
    Days of pleasure are like streams
    Through fair meadows gliding.
    Weal and woe, time doth go,
    Time is never turning:
    Secret fates guide our states,
    Both in mirth and mourning.

                     Thomas Campion

Chinese Burial Songs

(1)
'The dew on the garlic-leaf,' sung at the burial of kings and
princes.

    How swiftly it dries,
    The dew on the garlic-leaf!
    The dew that dries so fast
    To-morrow will fall again.
    But he whom we carry to the grave
    Will never more return.

(2)
'The Graveyard,' sung at the burial of common men.

What man's land is the graveyard?
It is the crowded home of ghosts –
Wise and foolish shoulder to shoulder.
The King of the Dead claims them all;
Man's fate knows no tarrying.

Translated Arthur Waley

Know then thyself, presume not God to scan;
The proper study of mankind is Man.
Placed on this isthmus of a middle state,
A being darkly wise and rudely great:
With too much knowledge for the Sceptic side,
With too much weakness for the Stoic's pride,
He hangs between; in doubt to act or rest,
In doubt to deem himself a God or Beast,
In doubt his mind or body to prefer;
Born but to die, and reasoning but to err;
Alike in ignorance, his reason such
Whether he thinks too little or too much:
Chaos of thought and passion, all confused;
Still by himself abused, or disabused;
Created half to rise and half to fall;
Great lord of all things, yet a prey to all;
Sole judge of truth, in endless error hurled:
The glory, jest, and riddle of the world!

Alexander Pope

What has this Bugbear Death to frighten Man,
If Souls can die, as well as Bodies can?
For, as before our Birth we felt no Pain,
When Punic arms infested Land and Main,
When Heaven and Earth were in confusion hurl'd,
For the debated Empire of the World,
Which aw'd with dreadful expectation lay,
Sure to be Slaves, uncertain who should sway:
So, when our mortal frame shall be disjoin'd,
The lifeless Lump uncoupled from the mind,
From sense of grief and pain we shall be free;
We shall not feel, because we shall not *Be* . . .
Nay, ev'n suppose when we have suffer'd Fate,
The Soul could feel, in her divided state,
What's that to us? for we are only we
While Souls and Bodies in one frame agree . . .
We, who are dead and gone, shall bear no part
In all the pleasures, nor shall feel the smart,
Which to that other Mortal shall accrue,
Whom, of our Matter Time shall mould anew.
For backward if you look, on that long space
Of Ages past, and view the changing face
Of Matter, toss'd and variously combin'd
In sundry shapes, 'tis easy for the mind
From thence t'infer, that Seeds of things have been
In the same order as they now are seen:
Which yet our dark remembrance cannot trace,
Because a pause of Life, a gaping space,
Has come betwixt, where memory lies dead,
And all the wand'ring motions from the sense are fled.
For whosoe'er shall in misfortunes live,
Must *Be*, when those misfortunes shall arrive;

And since the Man who *Is* not, feels not woe
(For death exempts him and wards off the blow,
Which we, the living, only feel and bear),
What is there left for us in Death to fear?
When once that pause of life has come between,
'Tis just the same as we had never been.

John Dryden (translation of *Lucretius: De Rerum Natura*)

'No Worst, there is None'

No worst, there is none. Pitched past pitch of grief,
More pangs will, schooled at forepangs, wilder wring.
Comforter, where, where is your comforting?
Mary, mother of us, where is your relief?
My cries heave, herds-long; huddle in a main, a chief-
    woe, world-sorrow; on an age-old anvil wince and
    sing –
Then lull, then leave off. Fury had shrieked 'No
    lingering! Let me be fell: force I must be brief'.
O the mind, mind has mountains; cliffs of fall
Frightful, sheer, no-man-fathomed. Hold them cheap
May who ne'er hung there. Nor does long our small
Durance deal with that steep or deep. Here! creep,
Wretch, under a comfort serves in a whirlwind: all
Life death does end and each day dies with sleep.

Gerard Manley Hopkins

My Epitaph

Below lies one whose name was traced in sand.
He died, not knowing what it was to live:
Died, while the first sweet consciousness of manhood
And maiden thought electrified his soul,
Faint beatings in the calyx of the rose.
Bewildered reader! pass without a sigh.
In a proud sorrow! There is life with God,
In other kingdom of a sweeter air.
In Eden every flower is blown. Amen.

David Gray

Enough! Why should a man bemoan
A Fate that leads the natural way?
Or think himself a worthier one
Than those who braved it in their day?
If only gladiators died,
Or heroes, Death would be his pride.
But have not little maidens gone,
And Lesbia's sparrow – all alone?

Oliver St. John Gogarty

His picture *The Ancient of Days* was such a favourite with Blake that three days before his death he sat up in bed and tinted it with his choicest colours. He touched and retouched it, held it at arm's length, and then threw it from him, exclaiming, *There! that will do! I cannot mend it!*

He saw his wife in tears; she felt this was to be the last of his works. 'Stay, Kate!' cried Blake, 'keep just as you are. I will draw your portrait, for you have been an angel to me.' She obeyed, and the dying artist made a fine likeness.

He lay chanting songs, and lamented that he could no longer commit these inspirations to paper. 'Kate,' he said, 'I am a changing man; I always rose and wrote down my thoughts, whether it rained, snowed, or shone, and you rose, too, and sat beside me; now this can be no longer.'

He died on August 12, and his wife, who sat watching him, did not perceive when he ceased breathing.

Allan Cunningham's *Life of Blake*

Jerusalem

And did those feet in ancient time
Walk upon England's mountains green?
And was the holy Lamb of God
On England's pleasant pastures seen?

And did the Countenance Divine
Shine forth upon our clouded hills?
And was Jerusalem builded here
Among these dark Satanic Mills?

Bring me my Bow of burning gold!
Bring me my Arrows of desire!
Bring me my Spear! O clouds, unfold!
Bring me my Chariot of fire!

I will not cease from Mental Fight,
Nor shall my Sword sleep in my hand,
Till we have built Jerusalem
In England's green and pleasant land.

William Blake

Death cancels everything but truth, and strips a man of everything but genius and virtue. It is a sort of natural canonization. It makes the meanest of us sacred; it installs the poet in his immortality, and lifts him to the skies. Death is the great assayer of the sterling ore of talent. At his touch the drossy particles fall off: the irritable, the personal, the gross, and mingle with the dust – the finer and more etherial part mounts with the winged spirit to watch over our latest memory, and protect our bones from insult. We consign the least worthy qualities to oblivion, and cherish the nobler and imperishable nature with double pride and fondness.

William Hazlitt: *The Spirit of the Age: Lord Byron*

And now what are we? unbelievers both,
Calm and complete, determinately fixed
To-day, to-morrow, and for ever, pray?
You'll guarantee me that? Not so, I think.
In no-wise! all we've gained is, that belief,
As unbelief before, shakes us by fits,
Confounds us like its predecessor. Where's
The gain? how can we guard our unbelief,
Make it bear fruit to us? – the problem here.
Just when we are safest, there's a sunset-touch,
A fancy from a flower-bell, some one's death,
A chorus-ending from Euripides, –
And that's enough for fifty hopes and fears
As old and new at once as Nature's self,
To rap and knock and enter in our soul,
Take hands and dance there, a fantastic ring,
Round the ancient idol, on his base again, –
The grand Perhaps! we look on helplessly, –
There the old misgivings, crooked questions are –
This good God, – what he could do, if he would,
Would, if he could – then must have done long since:
If so, when, where, and how? some way must be, –
Once feel about, and soon or late you hit
Some sense, in which it might be, after all.
Why not, 'The Way, the Truth, the Life?'

                    R. Browning: from *Bishop Blougram's Apology*

Dream-Pedlary

If there were dreams to sell,
    What would you buy?
Some cost a passing bell;
    Some a light sigh,
That shakes from Life's fresh crown
Only a roseleaf down.
If there were dreams to sell,
Merry and sad to tell,
And the crier rung the bell,
    What would you buy?

A cottage lone and still,
    With bowers nigh,
Shadowy, my woes to still,
    Until I die.
Such pearl from Life's fresh crown
Fain would I shake me down.
Were dreams to have at will,
This would best heal my ill,
    This would I buy.

But there were dreams to sell,
    Ill didst thou buy;
Life is a dream, they tell,
    Waking, to die.
Dreaming a dream to prize,
Is wishing ghosts to rise;
    And, if I had the spell
    To call the buried, well,
        Which one would I?

If there are ghosts to raise,
    What shall I call,
Out of hell's murky haze,
    Heaven's blue hall?
Raise my loved long-lost boy
To lead me to his joy.
    There are no ghosts to raise;
    Out of death lead no ways;
        Vain is the call.

Know'st thou not ghosts to sue?
    No love thou hast.
Else lie, as I will do,
    And breathe thy last.
So out of Life's fresh crown
Fall like a rose-leaf down.
    Thus are the ghosts to woo;
    Thus are all dreams made true,
        Ever to last!

                                        Thomas L. Beddoes

On Peaceful Death and Painful Life

Why dost thou sorrow for the happy dead?
    For, if their life be lost, their toils are o'er,
    And woe and want can trouble them no more;
Nor ever slept they in an earthly bed

So sound as now they sleep, while dreamless laid
   In the dark chambers of the unknown shore,
   Where Night and Silence guard each sealed door.
So, turn from such as these thy drooping head,
   And mourn the *Dead Alive* – whose spirit flies –
Whose life departs, before his death has come;
   Who knows no Heaven beneath Life's gloomy skies,
Who sees no Hope to brighten up that gloom, –
   'Tis *He* who feels the worm that never dies, –
The *real* death and darkness of the tomb.

Branwell Brontë

Song From the Waters

The swallow leaves her nest,
The soul my weary breast;
But therefore let the rain
   On my grave
Fall pure; for why complain?
Since both will come again
   O'er the wave.
The wind dead leaves and snow
Doth hurry to and fro;
And, once, a day shall break
   O'er the wave,

When a storm of ghosts shall shake
The dead until they wake
   In the grave.

                       Thomas L. Beddoes

I am going to do that which the dead oft promised he would do for me. This loved and loving brother, husband, father, friend, died where manhood's morning almost touches noon, and while the shadows still were falling toward the west. This brave and tender man in every storm of life was oak and rock; but in the sunshine he was vine and flower. He was the friend of all heroic souls. He climbed the heights and left all superstitions far below, while on his forehead fell the golden dawning of the grander day.

He loved the beautiful, and was with colour, form, and music touched to tears. He sided with the weak, the poor, and wronged, and lovingly gave alms. With loyal heart and with the purest hands he faithfully discharged all public trusts.

He was a worshipper of liberty, a friend of the oppressed. He added to the sum of human joy; and were every one to whom he did some loving service to bring a blossom to his grave, he would sleep tonight beneath a wilderness of flowers.

Life is a narrow vale between the cold and barren peaks of two eternities. We strive in vain to look beyond the heights. We cry aloud, and the only answer is the echo of our wailing cry. From the voiceless lips of the unreplying dead there comes no word; but in the night of death hope sees a star, and listening love can hear the rustle of a wing.

He who sleeps here, when dying, mistaking the approach of death for the return of health, whispered with his latest breath, *I am better now*. Let us believe, in spite of doubts and dogmas, of fears and tears, that these dear words are true of all the countlesss dead.

Robert G. Ingersoll at his brother's grave

The Comforters

When I crept over the hill, broken with tears,
    When I crouched down on the grass, dumb in
        despair,
I heard the soft croon of the wind bend to my ears,
    I felt the light kiss of the wind touching my hair.

When I stood lone on the height my sorrow did speak,
    As I went down the hill, I cried and I cried,
The soft little hands of the rain stroking my cheek,
    The kind little feet of the rain ran by my side.

When I went to thy grave, broken with tears,
    When I crouched down in the grass, dumb in despair,
I heard the sweet croon of the wind soft in my ears,
    I felt the kind lips of the wind touching my hair.

When I stood lone by thy cross, sorrow did speak,
   When I went down the long hill, I cried and I cried.
The soft little hands of the rain stroked my pale cheek,
   The kind little feet of the rain ran by my side.

                              Dora Sigerson Shorter

The Worldly Hope men set their Hearts upon
Turns Ashes – or it prospers; and anon,
   Like Snow upon the Desert's dusty Face,
Lighting a little hour or two – is gone.

Think, in this battered Caravanserai
Whose Portals are alternate Night and Day,
   How Sultan after Sultan with his Pomp
Abode his destined Hour, and went his way.

Ah, my Beloved, fill the Cup that clears
To-day of past Regrets and future Fears:
   To-morrow! – Why, To-morrow I may be
Myself with Yesterday's Seven thousand Years.

For some we loved, the loveliest and the best
That from his Vintage rolling Time hath prest,
   Have drunk their Cup a Round or two before,
And one by one crept silently to rest.

And we, that now make merry in the Room
They left, and Summer dresses in new bloom,
   Ourselves must we beneath the Couch of Earth
Descend – ourselves to make a Couch – for whom?

Ah, make the most of what we yet may spend,
Before we too into the Dust descend;
   Dust into Dust, and under Dust to lie,
Sans Wine, sans Song, sans Singer, and – sans End!

Edward Fitzgerald: from *The Rubaiyat of Omar Khayam*

There rolls the deep where grew the tree.
   O earth, what changes hast thou seen!
   There where the long street roars, hath been
The stillness of the central sea.

The hills are shadows, and they flow
   From form to form, and nothing stands;
   They melt like mist, the solid lands,
Like clouds they shape themselves and go.

But in my spirit will I dwell,
   And dream my dream, and hold it true;
   For though my lips may breathe adieu,
I cannot think the thing farewell.

Alfred, Lord Tennyson: from *In Memoriam*

Crossing alone the nighted ferry
With one coin for fee,
Whom, on the wharf of Lethe waiting
Count you to find? Not me.

The brisk fond lackey to fetch and carry,
The true, sick-hearted slave,
Expect him not in the just city
And free land of the grave.

A. E. Housman

Lost Land

Into my heart an air that kills
From you far country blows:
What are those blue remembered hills,
What spires, what farms are those?
That is the land of lost content,
I see it shining plain,
The happy highways where I went
And cannot come again.

A. E. Housman

Oh, come with old Khayyám, and leave the Wise
To talk; one thing is certain, that Life flies;
   One thing is certain, and the Rest is Lies;
The Flower that once has blown for ever dies.

Myself when young did eagerly frequent
Doctor and Saint, and heard great Argument
   About it and about: but evermore
Came out by the same Door as in I went.

With them the Seed of Wisdom did I sow,
And with my own hand labour'd it to grow:
   And this was all the Harvest that I reap'd –
'I came like Water, and like Wind I go.'

Into this Universe, and *why* not knowing,
Nor *whence*, like Water willy-nilly flowing:
   And out of it, as Wind along the Waste,
I know not *whither*, willy-nilly blowing.

What, without asking, hither hurried *whence!*
And, without asking, *whither* hurried hence!
   Another and another Cup to drown
The Memory of this Impertinence!

Up from Earth's Centre through the Seventh Gate
I rose, and on the Throne of Saturn sate,
   And many Knots unravel'd by the Road;
But not the Knot of Human Death and Fate.

Edward Fitzgerald: from *The Rubaiyat of Omar Khayam*

Parta Quies

Good-night; ensured release,
Imperishable peace,
   Have these for yours,
While sea abides, and land,
And earth's foundations stand,
And heaven endures.

When earth's foundations flee,
Nor sky nor land nor sea
   At all is found,
Content you, let them burn:
It is not your concern
Sleep on, sleep sound.

For nature, heartless, witless nature
   Will neither care nor know
What stranger's feet may find the meadow
   And trespass there and go,
Nor ask amid the dews of morning
If they are mine or no.

A. E. Housman

Where dwells that wish most ardent of the wise?
Too dark the sun to see it; highest stars
Too low to reach it; death, great death alone
O'er stars and sun, triumphant, lands us there
   Nor dreadful our transition tho' the mind
An artist at creating self-alarms
Rich in expedients for inquietude
Is prone to paint it dreadful. Who can take

Death's portrait true? The tyrant never sat.
Our sketch all random strokes, conjecture all;
Close shuts the grave, nor tells one single tale.
Death, and his image rising in the brain,
Bear faint resemblance; never are alike;
Fear shakes the pencil; fancy loves excess;
Dark ignorance is lavish of her shades:
And these the formidable picture draw.

                                        Edward Young

. . . Upon an everlasting tide
    Into the silent seas we go;
But verdure laughs along the side,
    And roses on the margin blow.

Nor life, nor death, nor aught they hold,
    Rate thou above their natural height;
Yet learn that all our eyes behold,
    Has value, if we mete it right.

Pluck then the flowers that line the stream,
    Instead of fighting with its power;
But pluck as flowers, not gems, nor deem
    That they will bloom beyond their hour.

Whate'er betides, from day to day,
    An even pulse and spirit keep;
And like a child, worn out with play,
    When wearied with existence, sleep.

        Sir Francis Hastings Doyle: from *The Epicurean*

Break, break, break,
  On thy cold gray stones, O Sea!
And I would that my tongue could utter
  The thoughts that arise in me.

O well for the fisherman's boy,
  That he shouts with his sister at play!
O well for the sailor lad,
  That he sings in his boat on the bay!

And the stately ships go on
  To their haven under the hill;
But O for the touch of a vanished hand,
  And the sound of a voice that is still!

Break, break, break,
  At the foot of thy crags, O Sea!
But the tender grace of a day that is dead
  Will never come back to me.

                                        Alfred, Lord Tennyson

Tears, Idle Tears

Tears, idle tears, I know not what they mean,
Tears from the depth of some divine despair
Rise in the heart, and gather to the eyes,
In looking on the happy Autumn-fields,
And thinking of the days that are no more.

Fresh as the first beam glittering on a sail,
That brings our friends up from the underworld,
Sad as the last which reddens over one
That sinks with all we love below the verge;
So sad, so fresh, the days that are no more.

Ah, sad and strange as in dark summer dawns
The earliest pipe of half-awakened birds
To dying ears, when unto dying eyes
The casement slowly grows a glimmering square;
So sad, so strange, the days that are no more.

Dear as remembered kisses after death,
And sweet as those by hopeless fancy feigned
On lips that are for others; deep as love,
Deep as first love, and wild with all regret;
O Death in Life, the days that are no more.

Alfred, Lord Tennyson

Epitaph

These are two friends whose lives were undivided;
So let their memory be, now they have glided
Under the grave; let not their bones be parted,
For their two hearts in life were single-hearted.

P. B. Shelley

O that 'twere possible,
   After long grief and pain,
To find the arms of my true-love
   Round me once again! . . .

A shadow flits before me –
   Not thou, but like to thee.
Ah God! that it were possible
   For one short hour to see
The souls we loved, that they might tell us
   What and where they be. . . .

                Alfred, Lord Tennyson

The Voice

Woman much missed, how you call to me, call to me,
Saying that now you are not as you were
When you had changed from the one who was all to
      me,
But as at first, when our day was fair.

Can it be you that I hear? Let me view you, then,
Standing as when I drew near to the town
Where you would wait for me: yes, as I knew you then
Even to the original air-blue gown!

Or is it only the breeze, in its listlessness
Travelling across the wet mead to me here,
You being ever dissolved to wan wistlessness,
Heard no more again far or near?

Thus I; faltering forward,
Leaves around me falling,
Wind oozing thin through the thorn from norward.
And the woman calling.

Thomas Hardy

Requiem

Under the wide and starry sky,
Dig the grave and let me lie.
Glad did I live and gladly die,
    And I laid me down with a will.

This be the verse you grave for me:
Here he lies where he longed to be;
Home is the sailor, home from sea,
    And the hunter home from the hill.

R. L. Stevenson

I am a part of all that I have met;
Yet all experience is an arch wherethrough
Gleams that untravelled world, whose margin fades
For ever and for ever when I move.
How dull it is to pause, to make an end,
To rust unburnished, not to shine in use!
As though to breathe were life. Life piled on life
Were all too little, and of one to me
Little remains: but every hour is saved
From that eternal silence, something more,
A bringer of new things; and vile it were
For some three suns to store and hoard myself,
And this gray spirit yearning in desire
To follow knowledge like a sinking star,
Beyond the utmost bound of human thought.

*   *   *

There lies the port; the vessel puffs her sail:
There gloom the dark broad seas. My mariners,
Souls that have toiled, and wrought, and thought with
        me –
That ever with a frolic welcome took
The thunder and the sunshine, and opposed
Free hearts, free foreheads – you and I are old;
Old age hath yet his honour and his toil;
Death closes all: but something ere the end,
Some work of noble note, may yet be done,
Not unbecoming men that strove with Gods.

*   *   *

The lights begin to twinkle from the rocks:
The long day wanes: the slow moon climbs: the deep
Moans round with many voices. Come, my friends,
'Tis not too late to seek a newer world.
Push off, and sitting well in order smite
The sounding furrows; for my purpose holds
To sail beyond the sunset, and the baths
Of all the western stars, until I die.
It may be that the gulfs will wash us down:
It may be we shall touch the Happy Isles,
And see the great Achilles, whom we knew.
Though much is taken, much abides; and though
We are not now that strength which in old days
Moved earth and heaven; that which we are, we are;
One equal temper of heroic hearts,
Made weak by time and fate, but strong in will
To strive, to seek, to find, and not to yield.

Alfred, Lord Tennyson: from *Ulysses*

Crossing the Bar

Sunset and evening star,
    And one clear call for me!
And may there be no moaning of the bar,
    When I put out to sea,

But such a tide as moving seems asleep,
    Too full for sound and foam,
When that which drew from out the boundless deep
    Turns again home.

Twilight and evening bell,
    And after that the dark!
And may there be no sadness of farewell,
    When I embark;

For though from out our bourne of Time and Place
    The flood may bear me far,
I hope to see my Pilot face to face
    When I have crost the bar.

                                        Alfred, Lord Tennyson

Or they loved their life through, and then went
            whither?
    And were one to the end – but what end who
            knows?
Love deep as the sea as a rose must wither,
    As the rose-red seaweed that mocks the rose.
Shall the dead take thought for the dead to love them?
    What love was ever as deep as a grave?
They are loveless now as the grass above them
            Or the wave.

All are at one now, roses and lovers,
   Not known of the cliffs and the fields and the sea.
Not a breath of the time that has been hovers
   In the air now soft with a summer to be.
Not a breath shall there sweeten the seasons hereafter
   Of the flowers or the lovers that laugh now or weep,
When as they that are free now of weeping and
       laughter
     We shall sleep.

Here death may deal not again for ever;
   Here change may come not till all change end.
From the graves they have made they shall rise up
       never,
   Who have left nought living to ravage and rend.
Earth, stones, and thorns of the wild ground growing,
   While the sun and the rain live, these shall be;
Till a last wind's breath upon all these blowing
     Roll the sea.

Till the slow sea rise and the sheer cliff crumble,
   Till terrace and meadow the deep gulfs drink,
Till the strength of the waves of the high tides humble
   The fields that lessen, the rocks that shrink,
Here now in his triumph where all things falter,
   Stretched out on the spoils that his own hand spread,
As a god self-slain on his own strange altar,
     Death lies dead.

       A. C. Swinburne: from *The Forsaken Garden*

We are not sure of sorrow,
And joy was never sure;
Today will die tomorrow;
Time stoops to no man's lure;
And love, grown faint and fretful,
With lips but half regretful
Sighs and with eyes forgetful
Weeps that no loves endure.

From too much love of living,
From hope and fear set free,
We thank with brief thanksgiving
Whatever gods may be
    That no life lives for ever;
    That dead men rise up never;
That even the weariest river
Winds somewhere safe to sea.

Then star nor sun shall waken,
Nor any change of light:
Nor sound of waters shaken,
Nor any sound or sight:
    Nor wintry leaves nor vernal,
    Nor days nor things diurnal;
Only the sleep eternal
    In an eternal night.

A. C. Swinburne: from *The Garden of Proserpine*

The Dislike of Death

We cannot like both life and death at once; no one can be expected to like two such opposite things at the same time; if we like life we must dislike death, and if we leave off disliking death we shall soon die. Death will always be more avoided than sought; for living involves effort, perceived or unperceived, central or departmental, and this will only be made by those who dislike the consequences of not making it more than the trouble of making it. A race, therefore, which is to exist at all must be a death-disliking race, for it is only at the cost of death that we can rid ourselves of all aversion to the idea of dying, so that the hunt after a philosophy which shall strip death of his terrors is like trying to find the philosopher's stone which cannot be found and which, if found, would defeat its own object.

Moreover, as a discovery which should rid us of the fear of death would be the vainest, so also it would be the most immoral of discoveries, for the very essence of morality is involved in the dislike (within reasonable limits) of death. Morality aims at a maximum of comfortable life and a minimum of death; if then, a minimum of death and a maximum of life were no longer held worth striving for, the whole fabric of morality would collapse, as indeed we have it on record that is is apt to do among classes that from one cause or another have come to live in disregard and expectation of death.

However much we may abuse death for robbing us of our friends – and there is no one who is not sooner or later hit hard in this respect – yet time heals these wounds sooner than we like to own; if the heyday of grief does not shortly kill outright, it passes; and I doubt whether most men, if they were to search their hearts, would not find that, could they command death for some single occasion, they would be more likely to bid him take than restore.

Moreover, death does not blight love as the accidents of time and life do. Even the fondest grow apart if parted; they cannot come together again, not in any closeness or for any long time. Can death do worse than this?

The memory of a love that has been cut short by death remains still fragrant though enfeebled, but no recollection of its past can keep sweet a love that has dried up and withered through accidents of time and life.

From the *Notebooks* of Samuel Butler

I. *Ignorance of Death*

i

The fear of death is instinctive because in so many past generations we have feared it. But how did we come to know what death is so that we should fear it? The answer is that we do not know what death is and that this is why we fear it.

ii

If a man know not life which he hath seen how shall he know death which he hath not seen?

iii

If a man has sent his teeth and his hair and perhaps two or three limbs to the grave before him, the presumption should be that, as he knows nothing further of these when they have once left him, so will he know nothing of the rest of him when it too is dead. The whole may surely be argued from the parts.

iv

To write about death is to write about that of which we have had little practical experience. We can write about conscious life, but we have no consciousness of the deaths we daily die. Besides, we cannot eat our cake and have it. We cannot have *tabulæ rasæ* and *tabulæ scriptæ* at the same time. We cannot be at once dead enough to be reasonably registered as such, and alive enough to be able to tell people all about it.

v

There will come a supreme moment in which there will be care neither for ourselves nor for others, but a complete abandon, a *sans souci* of unspeakable indifference, and this moment will never be taken from us; time cannot rob us of it but, as far as we are concerned, it will last for ever and ever without flying. So that, even for the most wretched and most guilty, there is a heaven at last where neither moth nor rust doth corrupt and where thieves do not break through nor steal. To himself every one is an immortal: he may know that he is going to die, but he can never know that he is dead.

vi

If life is an illusion, then so is death – the greatest of all illusions. If life must not be taken too seriously – then so neither must death.

vii

The dead are often just as living to us as the living are,
only we cannot get them to believe it. They can come to
us, but till we die we cannot go to them. To be dead is to
be unable to understand that one is alive.

From the *Notebooks* of Samuel Butler

II. *Dissolution*

Death is the dissolving of a partnership, the partners to
which survive and go elsewhere. It is the corruption or
breaking up of that society which we have called Ourself.
The corporation is at an end, both its soul and its body
cease as a whole, but the immortal constituents do not
cease and never will. The souls of some men transmigrate
in great part into their children, but there is a large alloy
in respect both of body and mind through sexual
generation; the souls of other men migrate into books,
pictures, music, or what not; and every one's mind
migrates somewhere, whether remembered and admired
or the reverse. The living souls of Handel, Shakespeare,
Rembrandt, Giovanni Bellini and the other great ones
appear and speak to us in their works with less alloy than
they could ever speak through their children; but men's
bodies disappear absolutely on death, except they be in
some measure preserved in their children and in so far as
harmonics of all that has been remain.

On death we do not lose life, we only lose
individuality; we live henceforth in others not in
ourselves. Our mistake has been in not seeing that death

is indeed, like birth, a salient feature in the history of the individual, but one which wants exploding as the end of the individual, no less than birth wanted exploding as his beginning.

Dying is only a mode of forgetting. We shall see this more easily if we consider forgetting to be a mode of dying. So the ancients called their River of Death, Lethe – the River of Forgetfulness. They ought also to have called their River of Life, Mnemosyne – the River of Memory. We should learn to tune death a good deal flatter than according to received notions.

From the *Notebooks* of Samuel Butler

Birth and Death

They are functions one of the other and if you get rid of one you must get rid of the other also. There is birth in death and death in birth. We are always dying and being born again.

Life is the gathering of waves to a head, at death they break into a million fragments each one of which, however, is absorbed at once into the sea of life and helps to form a later generation which comes rolling on till it too breaks.

Samuel Butler

We commonly know that we are going to die though we do not know that we are going to be born. But are we sure this is so? We may have had the most gloomy forebodings on this head and forgotten all about them. At any rate we know no more about the very end of our lives than about the very beginning. We come up unconsciously, and go down unconsciously; and we rarely see either birth or death. We see people, as consciousness, between the two extremes.

Samuel Butler

Teach me to live that I may dread
The grave as little as my bed.

This is from the evening hymn which all respectable children are taught. It sounds well, but it is immoral.

Our own death is a premium which we must pay for the far greater benefit we have derived from the fact that so many people have not only lived but also died before us. For if the old ones had not in course of time gone there would have been no progress; all our civilisation is due to the arrangement whereby no man shall live for ever, and to this huge mass of advantage we must each contribute our mite; that is to say, when our turn comes we too must die. The hardship is that interested persons should be able to scare us into thinking the change we call death to be the desperate business which they make it out to be. There is no hardship in having to suffer that change.

Bishop Ken, however, goes too far. Undesirable, of course, death must always be to those who are fairly well off, but it is undesirable that any living being should live in habitual indifference to death. The indifference should be kept for worthy occasions, and even then, though death be gladly faced, it is not healthy that it should be faced as though it were a mere undressing and going to bed.

Samuel Butler

Complete Death

To die completely, a person must not only forget but be forgotten, and he who is not forgotten is not dead. This is as old as *non omnis moriar* and a great deal older, but very few people realise it.

Life and Death

When I was young I used to think the only certain thing about life was that I should one day die. Now I think the only certain thing about life is that there is no such thing as death.

The Defeat of Death

There is nothing which at once affects a man so much and so little as his own death. It is a case in which the going-to-happen-ness of a thing is of greater importance than the actual thing itself which cannot be of importance to the man who dies, for Death cuts his own throat in the matter of hurting people. As a bee that can sting once but in the stinging dies, so Death is dead to him who is dead already.

Samuel Butler

Our Trivial Bodies

Though we think so much of our body, it is in reality a small part of us. Before birth we get together our tools, in life we use them, and thus fashion our true life which consists not in our tools and tool-box but in the work we have done with our tools. It is Handel's work, not the body with which he did the work, that pulls us half over London. There is not an action of a muscle in a horse's leg upon a winter's night as it drags a carriage to the Albert Hall but is in connection with, and part outcome of, the force generated when Handel sat in his room at Gopsall and wrote the *Messiah*. Think of all the forces which that force has controlled, and think, also, how small was the amount of molecular disturbance from which it proceeded. It is as though we saw a conflagration which a spark had kindled. This is the true Handel, who is a more living power among us [one hundred and twenty-two years after his death] than during the time he was amongst us in the body.

The whole life of some people is a kind of partial death – a long, lingering death-bed, so to speak, of stagnation and nonentity on which death is but the seal, or solemn signing, as the abnegation of all further act and deed on the part of the signer. Death robs these people of even that little strength which they appeared to have and gives them nothing but repose.

On others, again, death confers a more living kind of life than they can ever possibly have enjoyed while to those about them they seemed to be alive. Look at Shakespeare; can he be properly said to have lived in anything like his real life till a hundred years or so after his death? His physical life was but as a dawn preceding the sunrise of that life of the world to come which he was to enjoy hereafter. True, there was a little stir – a little abiding of shepherds in the fields, keeping watch over their flocks by night – a little buzzing in knots of men waiting to be hired before the daybreak – a little stealthy movement as of a burglar or two here and there – an inchoation of life. But the true life of the man was after death and not before it.

Death is not more the end of some than it is the beginning of others. So he that loses his soul may find it, and he that finds may lose it.

Notebooks of Samuel Butler

The Darkling Thrush

I leant upon a coppice gate
    When Frost was spectre-gray,
And Winter's dregs made desolate
    The weakening eye of day.
The tangled bine-stems scored the sky
    Like strings of broken lyres,
And all mankind that haunted nigh
    Had sought their household fires.

The land's sharp features seemed to be
    The Century's corpse outleant,
His crypt the cloudy canopy,
    The wind his death-lament.
The ancient pulse of germ and birth
    Was shrunken hard and dry,
And every spirit upon earth
    Seemed fervourless as I.

At once a voice arose among
    The bleak twigs overhead
In a full-hearted evensong
    Of joy illimited;
An aged thrush, frail, gaunt, and small,
    In blast-beruffled plume,
Had chosen thus to fling his soul
    Upon the growing gloom.

So little cause for carolings
    Of such ecstatic sound
Was written on terrestrial things
    Afar or nigh around,

> That I could think there trembled through
>   His happy goodnight air
> Some blessed Hope, whereof he knew
>   And I was unaware.

Thomas Hardy

I can of course appreciate your feelings about poor Kirk's funeral. Stripped of all wherewith belief and tradition have clothed it, death appears a little grimmer – a shade more chilly and loathsome – in the eyes of the most matter of fact. At the same time, while this is sad, it would have been not only sad but shocking to have pronounced over Kirk words that he did not believe and performed ceremonies which he himself would have denounced as meaningless. Yet, as you say, he is so stamped on one's mind, so often present in thought, that he makes his own acceptance and annihilation the more unthinkable. I have seen death fairly often and never yet been able to find it anything but extraordinary and rather incredible. The real person is so very real, so obviously living and different from what is left, that one cannot believe something has turned into nothing. It is not faith, is not reason – just a 'feeling' . . . .

C. S. Lewis to his Father on the death of
W. T. Kirkpatrick, 23 April 1921

A Wish for Unconsciousness

If I could but abide
As a tablet on a wall,
Or a hillock daisy-pied,
Or a picture in a hall,
And as nothing else at all,
I should feel no doleful achings,
I should hear no judgment-call,
Have no evil dreams or wakings,
No uncouth or grisly care;
In a word, no cross to bear.

                                        Thomas Hardy

In Tenebris

Wintertime nighs;
But my bereavement-pain
It cannot bring again:
    Twice no one dies.

Flower-petals flee;
But, since it once hath been,
No more that severing scene
    Can harrow me.

Birds faint in dread:
I shall not lose old strength
In the lone frost's black length:
    Strength long since fled!

> Leaves freeze to dun;
> But friends can not turn cold
> This season as of old
> For him with none.
>
> Tempests may scath;
> But love can not make smart
> Again this year his heart
> Who no heart hath.
>
> Black is night's cope;
> But death will not appal
> One who, past doubtings all,
> Waits in unhope.

Thomas Hardy

Clouds

Down the blue night the unending columns press
  In noiseless tumult, break and wave and flow,
  Now tread the far South, or lift rounds of snow
Up to the white moon's hidden loveliness.
Some pause in their grave wandering comradeless,
  And turn with profound gesture vague and slow,
  As who would pray good for the world, but know
Their benediction empty as they bless.

They say that the Dead die not, but remain
  Near to the rich heirs of their grief and mirth.
    I think they ride the calm mid-heaven, as these,

In wise majestic melancholy train,
    And watch the moon, and the still-raging seas,
And men, coming and going on the earth.

Rupert Brooke

Heredity

I am the family face;
Flesh perishes, I live on,
Projecting trait and trace
Through time to times anon,
And leaping from place to place
Over oblivion.

The years-heired feature that can
In curve and voice and eye
Despise the human span
Of durance – that is I;
The eternal thing in man,
That heeds no call to die.

Thomas Hardy

The Sunlight on the Garden

The sunlight on the garden
Hardens and grows cold,
We cannot cage the minute
Within its nets of gold,
When all is told
We cannot beg for pardon.

Our freedom as free lances
Advances towards its end;
The earth compels, upon it
Sonnets and birds descend;
And soon, my friend,
We shall have no time for dances.

The sky was good for flying
Defying the church bells
And every evil iron
Siren and what it tells;
The earth compels,
We are dying, Egypt, dying.

And not expecting pardon,
Hardened in heart anew,
But glad to have sat under
Thunder and rain with you,
And grateful too
For sunlight on the garden.

Louis Macneice

10

Some Characters of the Dead Remembered

How happy is he born and taught
    That serveth not another's will;
Whose armour is his honest thought,
    And simple truth his utmost skill!

Whose passions not his masters are,
    Whose soul is still prepared for death,
Not tied unto the world with care
    Of public fame, or private breath;

Who envies none that chance doth raise
    Or vice; who never understood
How deepest wounds are given by praise;
    Nor rules of state, but rules of good;

Who hath his life from rumours freed;
    Whose conscience is his strong retreat;
Whose state can neither flatterers feed,
    Nor ruin make accusers great;

Who God doth late and early pray
    More of His grace than gifts to lend;
And entertains the harmless day
    With a well-chosen book or friend:

This man is freed from servile bands
Of hope to rise, or fear to fall;
Lord of himself, though not of lands;
And, having nothing, yet hath all.

Sir Henry Wotton

Heights and Depths

He walked in glory on the hills;
We dalesmen envied from afar
   The heights and rose-lit pinnacles
   Which placed him nigh the evening star.

Upon the peaks they found him dead;
And now we wonder if he sighed
   For our low grass beneath his head,
   For our rude huts, before he died.

William Canton

If we consider her person, she was in the flower of her
age, of a temperate, plain and natural diet, without
curiosity or an intemperate palate; she spent less time in
dressing than many servants; her recreations were little
and seldom, her prayers often, her reading much: she
was of a most noble and charitable soul; a great lover of

honourable actions, and as great a despiser of base things; hugely loving to oblige others, and very unwilling to be in arrears to any upon the stock of courtesies and liberality; so free in all acts of favour, that she would not stay to hear herself thanked, as being unwilling that what good went from her to a needful or an obliged person should ever return to her again: she was an excellent friend, and hugely dear to very many, especially to the best and most discerning persons; to all that conversed with her, and could understand her great worth and sweetness: she was of an honourable, a nice, and tender reputation; and of the pleasures of this world, which were laid before her in heaps, she took a very small and inconsiderable share, as not loving to glut herself with vanity, or take her portion of good things here below.

Jeremy Taylor: from *The Funeral Sermon for Lady Carbery*

*   *   *

She had a strict and severe education, and it was one of God's graces and favours to her: for being the heiress of a great fortune, and living amongst the throng of persons in the sight of vanities and empty temptations, that is, in that part of the kingdom where greatness is too often expressed in great follies and great vices, God had provided a severe and angry education to chastise the forwardness of a young spirit and a fair fortune, that she might for ever be so far distant from a vice, that she might only see it and lothe it, but never taste of it, so much as to be put to her choice whether she be virtuous or no. God, intending to secure this soul to Himself, would not suffer the follies of the world to seize upon her by way of too near a trial or busy temptation.

She was married young; and besides her business of religion, seemed to be ordained in the providence of God to bring to this honourable family a part of a fair fortune, and to leave behind her a fairer issue, worth ten thousand times her portion: and as if this had been all the public business of her life, when she had so far served God's ends, God in mercy would also serve hers, and take her to an early blessedness.

In passing through which line of providence, she had the art to secure her eternal interest, by turning her condition into duty, and expressing her duty in the greatest eminency of a virtuous, prudent, and rare affection, that hath been known in any example. . . .

. . . But if we examine how she demeaned herself towards God, there also you will find her not of a common, but of an exemplar piety. She was a great reader of scripture, confining herself to great portions every day; which she read not to the purposes of vanity and impertinent curiosities, not to seem knowing or to become talking, not to expound and rule; but to teach her all her duty, to instruct her in the knowledge and love of God and of her neighbours; to make her more humble, and to teach her to despise the world and all its gilded vanities; and that she might entertain passions wholly in design and order to heaven. I have seen a female religion that wholly dwelt upon the face and tongue; that like a wanton and an undressed tree spends all its juice in suckers and irregular branches, in leaves and gum, and after all such goodly outsides you should never eat an apple, or be delighted with the beauties or the perfumes of a hopeful blossom. But the religion of this excellent lady was of another constitution; it took root downward in humility, and brought forth fruit upward in the substantial graces of a Christian, in charity and justice, in chastity and modesty, in fair friendships and sweetness of society. She had not very much of the forms and outsides of godliness, but she was hugely careful for the power of it, for the moral, essential, and useful parts; such which would make her be, not seem to be, religious. . . .

. . . She was a very constant person at her prayers, and spent all her time which nature did permit to her choice, in her devotions, and reading and meditating, and the necessary offices of household government; every one of which is an action of religion, some by nature, some by adoption.

Jeremy Taylor: from *The Funeral Sermon for Lady Carbery*

In all her Religion, and in all her actions of relation towards God, she had a strange evenness and untroubled passage, sliding towards her ocean of God and of infinity with a certain and silent motion. So have I seen a river deep and smooth passing with a still foot and a sober face, and paying to the *Fiscus*, the great Exchequer of the Sea, the Prince of all the watery bodies, a tribute large and full: and hard by it a little brook skipping and making a noise upon its unequal and neighbour bottom; and after all its talking and bragging motion, it paid to its common Audit no more than the revenues of a little cloud, or a contemptible vessel: So have I sometimes compared the issues of her religion to the solemnities and fam'd outsides of another's piety. It dwelt upon her spirit, and was incorporated with the periodical work of every day: she did not believe that religion was intended to minister to fame and reputation, but to pardon of sins, to the pleasure of God, and the salvation of souls. For religion is like the breath of Heaven; if it goes abroad into the open air, it scatters and dissolves like camphyre: but if it enters into a secret hollowness, into a close conveyance, it is strong and mighty, and comes forth with vigour and great effect at the other end, at the other side of this life, in the days of death and judgment.

The other appendage of her religion, which also was a great ornament to all the parts of her life, was a rare modesty and humility of spirit, a confident despising and undervaluing of herself. For though she had the greatest judgment, and the greatest experience of things and persons that I ever yet knew in a person of her youth, and sex, and circumstances; yet as if she knew nothing of it, she had the meanest opinion of herself; and like a fair taper, when she shined to all the room, yet round about her own station she had cast a shadow and a cloud, and she shined to every body but herself. But the perfectness of her prudence and excellent parts could not be hid; and all her humility and arts of concealment, made the virtues more amiable and illustrious. For as pride sullies the beauty of the fairest virtues, and makes our understanding but like the craft and learning of a devil: so humility is the greatest eminency and art of publication in the whole world; and she in all her arts of secrecy and hiding her worthy things, was but 'like one that hideth the wind, and covers the ointment of her right hand.'

Jeremy Taylor:
from *The Funeral Sermon for Lady Carbery*

Integer Vitae

The man of life upright,
　　Whose guiltless heart is free
From all dishonest deeds
　　Or thought of vanity:

The man whose silent days
　　In harmless joys are spent,
Whom hopes cannot delude,
　　Nor sorrow discontent:

That man needs neither towers
　　Nor armour for defence,
Nor secret vaults to fly
　　From thunder's violence.

He only can behold
　　With unaffrighted eyes
The horrors of the deep
　　And terrors of the skies.

Thus scorning all the cares
　　That fate or fortune brings,
He makes the heaven his book,
　　His wisdom heavenly things,

Good thoughts his only friends,
　　His wealth a well-spent age,
The earth his sober inn
　　And quiet pilgrimage.

Thomas Campion

The Things That Matter

Now that I've nearly done my days,
  And grown too stiff to sweep or sew,
I sit and think, till I'm amaze,
  About what lots of things I know:
Things as I've found out one by one –
  And when I'm fast down in the clay,
My knowing things and how they're done
  Will all be lost and thrown away.

There's things, I know, as won't be lost,
  Things as folks write and talk about:
The way to keep your roots from frost,
  And how to get your ink spots out.
What medicine's good for sores and sprains,
  What way to salt your butter down,
What charms will cure your different pains,
  And what will bright your faded gown.

But more important things than these,
  They can't be written in a book:
How fast to boil your greens and peas,
  And how good bacon ought to look;
The feel of real good wearing stuff,
  The kind of apple as will keep,
The look of bread that's rose enough,
  And how to get a child asleep.

Whether the jam is fit to pot,
  Whether the milk is going to turn,
Whether a hen will lay or not,
  Is things as some folks never learn.

I know the weather by the sky,
    I know what herbs grow in what lane;
And if sick men are going to die,
    Or if they'll get about again.

Young wives come in, a-smiling, grave,
    With secrets that they itch to tell:
I know what sort of times they'll have,
    And if they'll have a boy or gell.
And if a lad is ill to bind,
    Or some young maid is hard to lead,
I know when you should speak 'em kind,
    And when it's scolding as they need.

I used to know where birds ud set,
    And likely spots for trout or hare,
And God may want me to forget
    The way to set a line or snare;
But not the way to truss a chick,
    To fry a fish, or baste a roast,
Nor how to tell, when folks are sick,
    What kind of herb will ease them most!

Forgetting seems such silly waste!
    I know so many little things,
And now the Angels will make haste
    To dust it all away with wings!
O God, you made me like to know,
    You kept the things straight in my head,
Please God, if you can make it so,
    Let me know *something* when I'm dead.

E. Nesbit

Of My Dear Son, Gervase Beaumont

Can I, who have for others oft compiled
The songs of Death, forget my sweetest child,
Which, like a flower crushed, with a blast is dead,
And ere full time hangs down his smiling head,
Expecting with clear hope to live anew
Among the angels, fed with heavenly dew?
We have this sign of joy, that many days,
While on the earth his struggling spirit stays,
The name of Jesus in his mouth contains
His only food, his sleep, his ease from pains.
O may that sound be rooted in my mind,
Of which in him such strong effect I find.
Dear Lord, receive my son, whose winning love
To me was like a friendship, far above
The course of nature or his tender age,
Whose looks could all my bitter griefs assuage;
Let his pure soul ordained seven years to be
In that frail body, which was part of me,
Remain my pledge in Heaven, as sent to show
How to this port at every step I go.

Sir John Beaumont

*An Epitaph upon Husband and Wife Who Died
and were Buried Together*

To those whom death again did wed
This grave's the second marriage-bed.
For though the hand of Fate could force
'Twixt soul and body a divorce,
It could not sever man and wife,
Because they both lived but one life.
Peace, good reader, do not weep;
Peace, the lovers are asleep.
They, sweet turtles, folded lie
In the last knot that love could tie.
Let them sleep, let them sleep on,
Till this stormy night be gone,
And the eternal morrow dawn;
Then the curtains will be drawn,
And they wake into a light
Whose day shall never die in night.

Richard Crashaw

On the Death of Mr. William Harvey

It was a dismal and a fearful night,
Scarce could the morn drive on the unwilling light,
When Sleep, Death's image, left my troubled breast
     By something liker Death possest.
My eyes with tears did uncommanded flow,
     And on my soul hung the dull weight
     Of some intolerable fate.
What bell was that? Ah me! too much I know.

My sweet companion, and my gentle peer,
Why hast thou left me thus unkindly here,
Thy end forever, and my life to moan?
    O thou hast left me all alone!
Thy soul and body, when death's agony
    Besieged around thy noble heart,
    Did not with more reluctance part
Than I, my dearest Friend, do part from thee.

My dearest Friend, would I had died for thee!
Life and this world henceforth will tedious be.
Nor shall I know hereafter what to do
    If once my griefs prove tedious too.
Silent and sad I walk about all day,
    As sullen ghosts stalk speechless by
    Where their hid treasures lie;
Alas, my treasure's gone, why do I stay?

He was my friend, the truest friend on earth;
A strong and mighty influence joined our birth.
Nor did we envy the most sounding name
    By Friendship given of old to Fame.
None but his brethren he, and sisters, knew
    Whom the kind youth preferred to me;
    And even in that we did agree,
For much above myself I loved them too.

Say, for you saw us, ye immortal lights,
How oft unwearied have we spent the nights,
Till the Ledaean stars, so famed for love,
    Wondered at us from above?
We spent them not in toys, in lusts, or wine,
    But search of deep Philosophy,
    Wit, Eloquence, and Poetry,
Arts which I loved, for they, my Friend, were thine.

Ye fields of Cambridge, our dear Cambridge, say,
Have ye not seen us walking every day?
Was there a tree about which did not know
    The love betwixt us two?
Henceforth, ye gentle trees, forever fade;
    Or your sad branches thicker join
    And into darksome shades combine,
Dark as the grave wherein my friend is laid. . . .

                         Abraham Cowley

On the Death of Mr. Robert Levet A Practiser in Physic

    Condemned to Hope's delusive mine,
      As on we toil from day to day,
    By sudden blasts or slow decline
      Our social comforts drop away.

    Well tried through many a varying year,
      See Levet to the grave descend;
    Officious, innocent, sincere,
      Of every friendless name the friend.

    Yet still he fills affection's eye,
      Obscurely wise and coarsely kind;
    Nor, lettered Arrogance, deny
      Thy praise to merit unrefined.

    When fainting nature called for aid,
      And hovering death prepared the blow,
    His vigorous remedy displayed
      The power of art without the show.

In Misery's darkest cavern known,
    His useful care was ever nigh,
Where hopeless Anguish poured his groan,
    And lonely Want retired to die.

No summons mocked by chill delay,
    No petty gain disdained by pride;
The modest wants of every day
    The toil of every day supplied.

His virtues walked their narrow round,
    Nor made a pause, nor left a void;
And sure the Eternal Master found
    The single talent well employed.

The busy day, the peaceful night,
    Unfelt, uncounted, glided by;
His frame was firm – his powers were bright,
    Though now his eightieth year was nigh.

Then with no fiery throbbing pain,
    No cold gradations of decay,
Death broke at once the vital chain,
    And freed his soul the nearest way.

Samuel Johnson

To a good Man of most dear memory
This Stone is sacred. Here he lies apart
From the great city where he first drew breath,
Was reared and taught; and humbly earned his bread,
To the strict labours of the merchant's desk
By duty chained. Not seldom did those tasks
Tease, and the thought of time so spent depress,
His spirit, but the recompense was high;
Firm Independence, Bounty's rightful sire;
Affections, warm as sunshine, free as air;
And when the precious hours of leisure came,
Knowledge and wisdom, gained from converse sweet
With books, or while he ranged the crowded streets
With a keen eye, and overflowing heart:
So genius triumped over seeming wrong,
And poured out truth in works by thoughtful love
Inspired – works potent over smiles and tears,
And as round mountain tops the lightning plays,
Thus innocently sported, breaking forth
As from a cloud of some grave sympathy,
Humour and wild instinctive wit, and all
The vivid flashes of his spoken words.
From the most gentle creature nursed in fields
Had been derived the name he bore – a name
Wherever Christian altars have been raised,
Hallowed to meekness and to innocence;
And if in him meekness at times gave way,
Provoked out of herself by troubles strange,
Many and strange, that hung about his life;
Still, at the centre of his being, lodged
A soul by resignation sanctified:
And if too often, self-reproached, he felt
That innocence belongs not to our kind,

A power that never ceased to abide in him,
Charity, mid the multitude of sins
That she can cover, left not his exposed
To an unforgiving judgment from just Heaven.
O, he was good, if e'er a good Man lived!

                    Wordsworth's epitaph on Charles Lamb

It is enough; the end and the beginning
    Are one thing to thee, who art past the end.
    O hand unclasped of unbeholden friend,
For thee no fruits to pluck, no palms for winning,
    No triumph and no labour and no lust,
    Only dead yew-leaves and a little dust.
O quiet eyes wherein the light saith nought,
    Whereto the day is dumb, nor any night
    With obscure finger silences your sight,
Nor in your speech the sudden soul speaks thought,
    Sleep, and have sleep for light.

Not thee, O never thee, in all time's changes,
    Not thee but this the sound of thy sad soul,
    The shadow of thy swift spirit, this shut scroll
I lay my hand on, and not death estranges
    My spirit from communion of thy song –
    These memories, and these melodies that throng
Veiled porches of a Muse funereal –
    These I salute, these touch, these clasp and fold
    As though a hand were in my hand to hold,
Or through mine ears a mourning musical
    Of many mourners rolled.

Therefore he too now at thy soul's sunsetting
   God of all suns and songs, he too bends down
   To mix his laurel with the cypress crown,
And save thy dust from blame and from forgetting.
   Therefore he too, seeing all thou wert and art,
   Compassionate with sad and sacred heart
Mourns thee of his many children the last dead,
   And hallows with strange tears and alien sighs.
   Thine unmelodious mouth and sunless eyes
And over thine irrevocable head
   Sheds light from the under skies.

For thee, O now a silent soul, my brother,
   Take at my hands this garland, and farewell.
   Thin is the leaf, and chill the wintry smell,
And chill the solemn earth, a fatal mother,
   With sadder than the Niobean womb,
   And in the hollow of her breasts a tomb.
Content thee, howso'er, whose days are done;
   There lies not any troublous thing before,
   Nor sight nor sound to war against thee more,
For whom all winds are quiet as the sun,
   All waters as the shore.

                 A. C. Swinburne: from 'Ave Atque Vale',
                   in memory of Charles Bandelaire

Forty years back, when much had place
That since has perished out of mind,
I heard that voice and saw that face.

He spoke as one afoot will wind
A morning horn ere men awake;
His note was trenchant, turning kind.

He was of those whose wit can shake
And riddle to the very core
The counterfeits that Time will break.

Of late, when we two met once more,
The luminous countenance and rare
Shone just as forty years before.

So that, when now all tongues declare
His shape unseen by his green hill,
I scarce believe he sits not there.

No matter. Further and further still
Through the world's vapourous, vitiate air
His words wind on – as live words will.

Thomas Hardy (on George Meredith)

11

Time

When I do count the clock that tells the time,
And see the brave day sunk in hideous night;
When I behold the violet past prime,
And sable curls all silver'd o'er with white;
When lofty trees I see barren of leaves,
Which erst from heat did canopy the herd,
And summer's green all girded up in sheaves,
Borne on the bier with white and bristly beard,
Then of thy beauty do I question make,
That thou among the wastes of time must go,
Since sweets and beauties do themselves forsake
And die as fast as they see others grow;
    And nothing 'gainst Time's scythe can make
      defence
    Save breed, to brave him when he takes thee
      hence.

William Shakespeare

Not marble, nor the gilded monuments
   Of princes, shall outlive this powerful rhyme;
But you shall shine more bright in these contents
   Than unswept stone, besmeared with sluttish time.
When wasteful war shall statues overturn,
   And broils root out the work of masonry,
Nor Mars his sword nor war's quick fire shall burn
   The living record of your memory.
'Gainst death and all oblivious enmity
   Shall you pace forth; your praise shall still find room
Even in the eyes of all posterity
   That wear this word out to the ending doom.
     So, till the judgement that yourself arise,
     You live in this, and dwell in lovers' eyes.

                          William Shakespeare

Like as the waves make towards the pebbled shore,
   So do our minutes hasten to their end;
Each changing place with that which goes before,
   In sequent toil all forwards do contend.
Nativity, once in the main of light,
   Crawls to maturity, wherewith being crowned,
Crooked eclipses 'gainst his glory fight,
   And Time that gave doth now his gift confound.
Time doth transfix the flourish set on youth
   And delves the parallels in beauty's brow,
Feeds on the rarities of nature's truth,
   And nothing stands but for his scythe to mow.
     And yet to times in hope my verse shall stand,
     Praising thy worth, despite his cruel hand.

                          William Shakespeare

When I have seen by Time's fell hand defaced
   The rich proud cost of outworn buried age;
When sometime lofty towers I see down razed,
   And brass eternal slave to mortal rage;
When I have seen the hungry ocean gain
   Advantage on the kingdom of the shore,
And the firm soil win of the watery main,
   Increasing store with loss, and loss with store;
When I have seen such interchange of state,
   Or state itself confounded to decay,
Ruin hath taught me thus to ruminate,
   That Time will come and take my Love away.
      This thought is as a death, which cannot choose
      But weep to have that which it fears to lose.

                      William Shakespeare

When I consider every thing that grows
 Holds in perfection but a little moment,
 That this huge stage presenteth nought but shows
 Whereon the stars in secret influence comment;
When I perceive that men as plants increase,
 Cheered and check'd even by the self-same sky,
 Vaunt in their youthful sap, at height decrease,
 And wear their brave state out of memory;
Then the conceit of this inconstant stay
 Sets you most rich in youth before my sight,
 Where wasteful Time debateth with Decay,
 To change your day of youth to sullied night;
      And all in war with Time for love of you,
      As he takes from you, I engraft you new.

                      William Shakespeare

Ah! Sunflower

Ah, Sunflower! weary of time,
Who countest the steps of the Sun,
Seeking after that sweet golden clime
Where the traveller's journey is done:

Where the Youth pined away with desire,
And the pale Virgin shrouded in snow
Arise from their graves, and aspire
Where my Sunflower wishes to go.

William Blake

Birthright

Lord Rameses of Egypt sighed
    Because a summer evening passed;
And little Ariadne cried
    That summer fancy fell at last
To dust; and young Verona died
    When beauty's hour was overcast.

Theirs was the bitterness we know
    Because the clouds of hawthorn keep
So short a state, and kisses go
    To tombs unfathomably deep,
While Rameses and Romeo
    And little Ariadne sleep.

John Drinkwater

Since brass, nor stone, nor earth, nor boundless sea,
　　But sad mortality o'ersways their power,
How with this rage shall beauty hold a plea,
　　Whose action is no stronger than a flower?
O, how shall summer's honey breath hold out
　　Against the wrackful siege of battering days,
When rocks impregnable are not so stout,
　　Nor gates of steel so strong, but Time decays?
O fearful meditation! Where, alack,
　　Shall Time's best jewel from Time's chest lie hid?
Or what strong hand can hold his swift foot back?
　　Or who his spoil of beauty can forbid?
　　　　O, none, unless this miracle have might,
　　　　That in black ink my love may still shine bright.

                                    William Shakespeare

So passeth in the passing of a day,
Of mortall life the leafe, the bud, the flowre;
No more doth flourish after first decay
That earst was sought to deck both bed and bowre
Of many a lady', and many a Paramowre.
Gather therefore the Rose whilest yet is prime,
For soon comes age that will her pride deflowre;
Gather the Rose of Love whilest yet is time,
Whilest loving thou mayest loved be with equal crime.

                    Edmund Spenser: from the *Faerie Queene*

Cities and Thrones and Powers
   Stand in Time's eye,
Almost as long as flowers,
   Which daily die:
But, as new buds put forth
   To glad new men,
Out of the spent and unconsidered Earth
   The Cities rise again.

This season's Daffodil
   She never hears
What change, what chance, what chill,
   Cut down last year's;
But with bold countenance,
   And knowledge small,
Esteems her seven days' continuance
   To be perpetual.

So Time that is o'erkind
   To all that be,
Ordains us e'en as blind,
   As bold as she:
That in our very death,
   And burial sure,
Shadow to shadow, well persuaded, saith,
   'See how our works endure!'

                    Rudyard Kipling

The seas are quiet when the winds give o'er;
So calm are we when passions are no more.
For then we know how vain it was to boast
Of fleeting things, so certain to be lost.
Clouds of affection from our younger eyes
Conceal that emptiness which age descries.

The soul's dark cottage, battered and decayed,
Lets in new light through chinks that Time has made
Stronger, by weakness, wiser men become
As they draw near to their eternal home.
Leaving the old, both worlds at once they view
That stand upon the threshold of the new.

Edmund Waller: from *Last Verses*

12

Lines for Private Meditation

Since we stay not here, being people but of a daye's abode, and our age is like that of a flie, and contemporary with a gourd, we must look somewhere else for an abiding city, a place in another country to fix our house in . . .   (Jeremy Taylor)

And life is given to none freehold, but it is leasehold for all.   (Lucretius)

Death joins us to the great majority.   (E. Young)

For death is not only saying farewell to the world and to all that we love, but also saying farewell to ourselves.
                                                    (Anon.)

This world nis but a thurghfare of wo,
And we ben pilgrimes, passing to and fro.
                (Geoffrey Chaucer: *The Knightes Tale*)

Canst thou by searching find out God?
                            (Wisdom of Solomon)

Death destroys a man; the idea of death saves him.
                            (E. M. Forster)

The sense of death is most in apprehension.
                (Shakespeare: *Measure for Measure*)

Were there but a few hearts and intellects like hers, this earth would already become the hoped-for heaven.

> (John Stuart Mill – Epitaph for his wife Harriet
> in the cemetery near Avignon)

While the child was yet alive I fasted and wept; but being now dead, why should I fast? Can I bring him again? I shall go to him, but he cannot return to me.

> (Bible A.V., 2. Sam. 22)

We owe respect to the living; to the dead we owe only truth.   (Voltaire)

All men think all men mortal but themselves. (E. Young)

> Death is the veil which those who live call life;
> They sleep, and it is lifted.

Lift not the painted veil which those who live call life.

> (Shelley)

I was not. I have been. I am not. I do not mind.

> (Epicurean epitaph)

> I was not, and was conceived.
> I loved, and did a little work.
> I am not, and grieve not.'   (W. K. Clifford)

> I fall asleep in the full and certain hope
> That my slumber shall not be broken;
> And that though I be all-forgetting,
> Yet shall I not be all-forgotten,
> But continue that life in the thoughts and deeds
> Of those I loved, . . .   (Samuel Butler)

Some races increase, others are reduced, and in a short while the generations of living creatures are changed and like runners relay the torch of life.

(Lucretius: *De Rerum Natura*)

We can know that there is nothing to be feared in death, that one who is not cannot be made unhappy, and that it matters not a scrap whether one might ever have been born at all, when death that is immortal has taken over one's mortal life . . .

Death therefore is nothing to us nor does it concern us a scrap, seeing that the nature of the spirit we possess is something mortal. (Lucretius: *De Rerum Natura*)

Oh how quickly the world's glory passes away.

(T. à Kempis)

We die alone.

(Pascal)

The eternal silence of those infinite spaces terrifies me.

(Pascal)

For man proposes, but God disposes. (T. à Kempis)

Anyone can stop a man's life, but no one his death; a thousand doors open on to it. (Seneca)

Lie urn by urn, and touch but in their names.

(Sir Thomas Browne: *Urn-burial*)

I would rather sleep in the southern corner of a little country churchyard, than in the tomb of the Capulets. I should like, however, that my dust should mingle with kindred dust. (Edmund E. Burke)

The rest is silence.

(Shakespeare)

Blank Pages Left for Personal Choices

Index of Sources

Index of First Lines

U

V